1942
1944
TAGES
BEHFEL

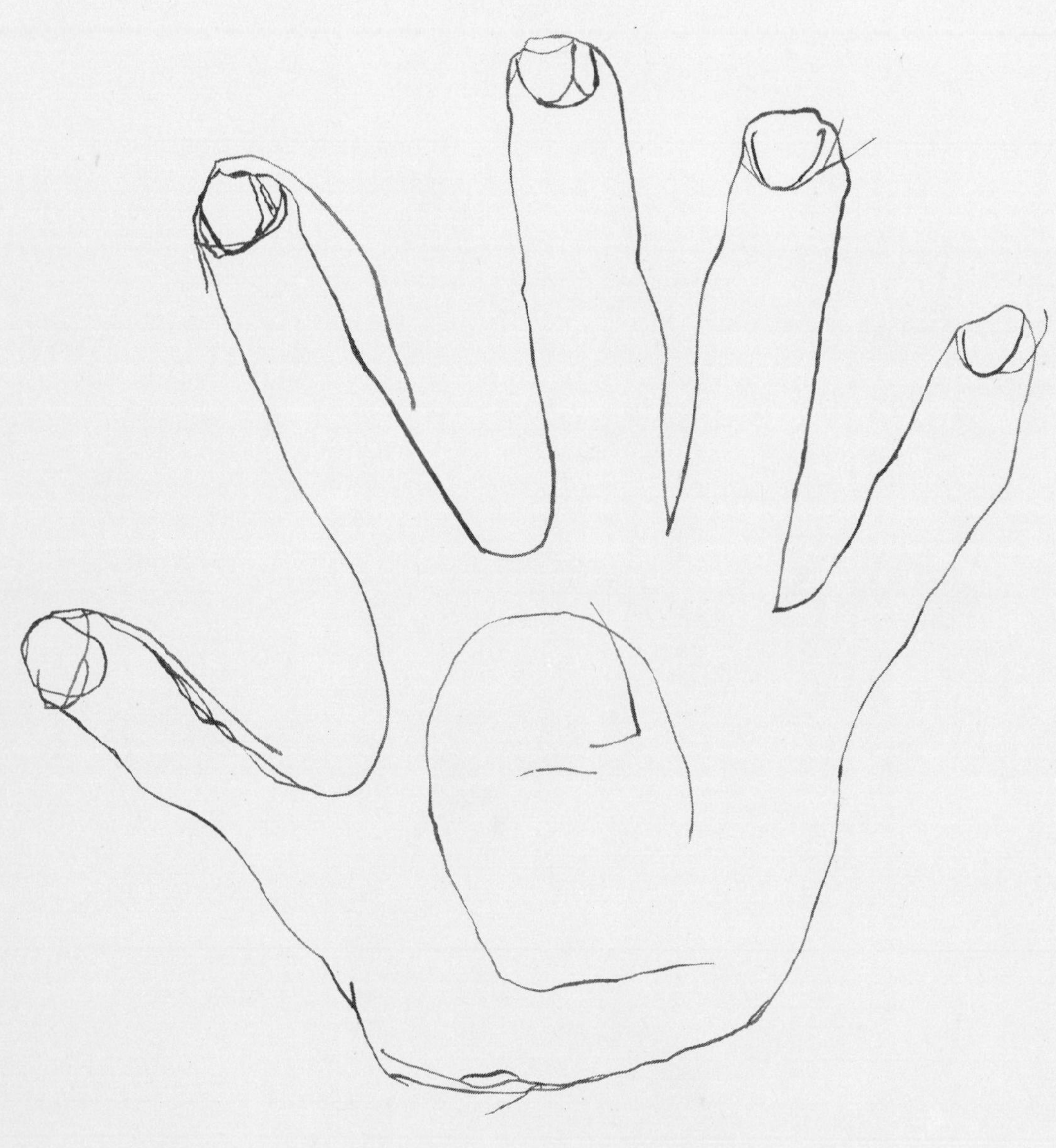

...I never saw another butterfly...

Children's Drawings and Poems from Terezín Concentration Camp 1942-1944

SCHOCKEN BOOKS • NEW YORK

First published by SCHOCKEN BOOKS 1978

Library of Congress Cataloging in Publication Data
Prague. Státní židovské museum.
I never saw another butterfly.

Translation of Dětské kresby na zastávce k smrti, Terezín, 1942–1944.
1. Children's art. 2. Children's writings.
3. Terezín (Concentration Camp) I. Volavková, Hana.
II. Title. III. Title: Children's drawings and poems
from Terezín Concentration Camp, 1942–1944.
N352.P713 1978 741.9'437'1 78-3542

Printed in Czechoslovakia
by Polygrafia, Prague

...only I never saw another butterfly....

AT TEREZÍN

When a new child comes
Everything seems strange to him.
What, on the ground I have to lie?
Eat black potatoes? No! Not I!
I've got to stay? It's dirty here!
The floor — why, look, it's dirt, I fear!
And I'm supposed to sleep on it?
I'll get all dirty!

Here the sound of shouting, cries,
And oh, so many flies.
Everyone knows flies carry disease.
Oooh, something bit me! Wasn't that a bedbug?
Here in Terezín, life is hell
And when I'll go home again, I can't yet tell.

"*Teddy*"
L 410 . 1943

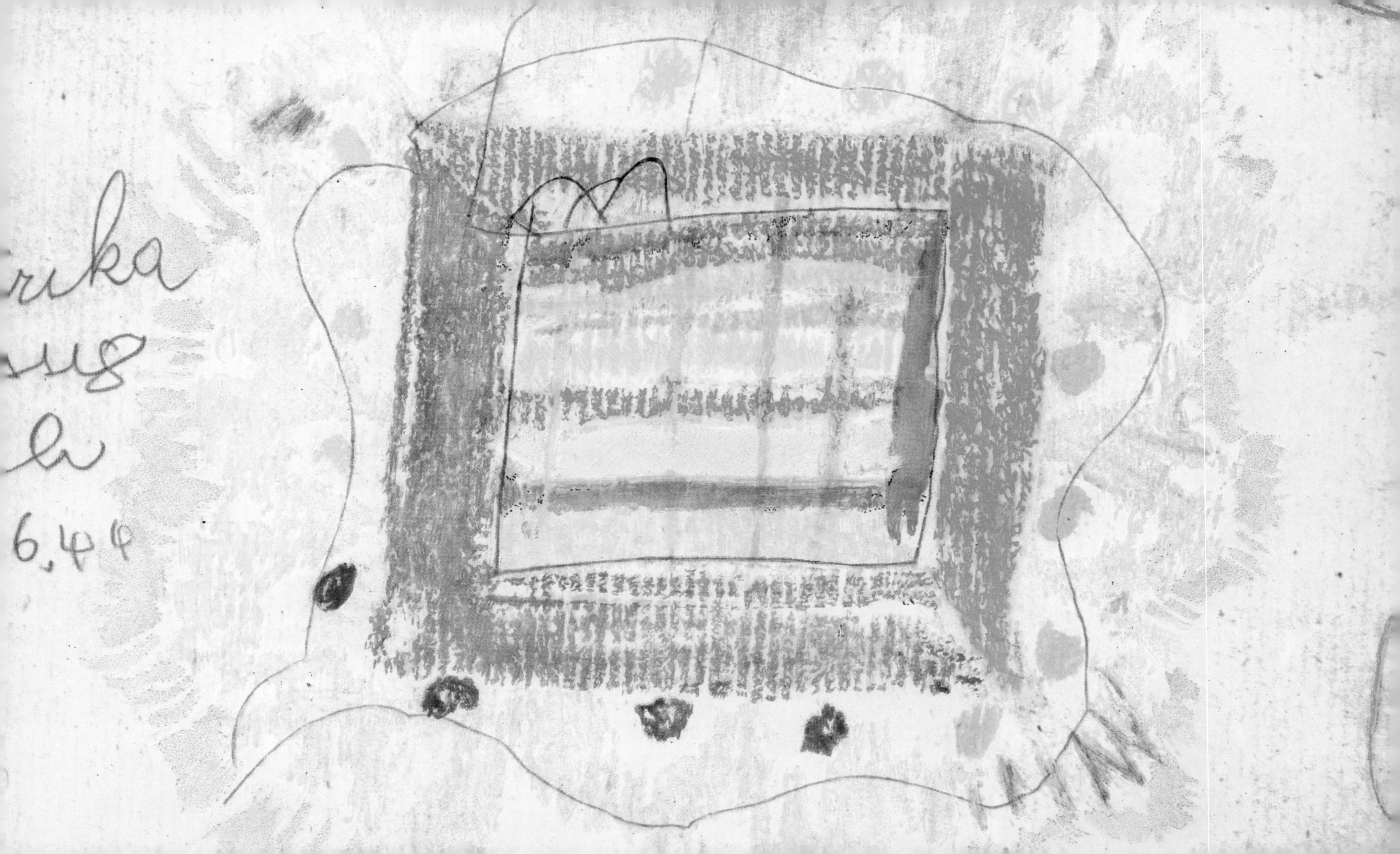
6,44

THE CLOSED TOWN

Everything leans, like tottering, hunched old women.

Every eye shines with fixed waiting
and for the word, "when"?

Here there are few soldiers.
Only the shot-down birds tell of war.

You believe every bit of news you hear.

The buildings now are fuller,
Body smelling close to body,
And the garrets scream with light for long, long hours.

This evening I walked along the street of death.
On one wagon, they were taking the dead away.

Why so many marches have been drummed here?

Why so many soldiers?

Then
A week after the end,
Everything will be empty here.
A hungry dove will peck for bread.
In the middle of the street will stand
An empty, dirty
Hearse.

Anonymous

. . . We got used to standing in line at 7 o'clock in the morning, at 12 noon and again at seven o'clock in the evening. We stood in a long queue with a plate in our hand, into which they ladled a little warmed-up water with a salty or a coffee flavor. Or else they gave us a few potatoes. We got used to sleeping without a bed, to saluting every uniform, not to walk on the sidewalks and then again to walk on the sidewalks. We got used to undeserved slaps, blows and executions. We got accustomed to seeing people die in their own excrement, to seeing piled-up coffins full of corpses, to seeing the sick amidst dirt and filth and to seeing the helpless doctors. We got used to it that from time to time, one thousand unhappy souls would come here and that, from time to time, another thousand unhappy souls would go away . . .

From the prose of 15 year old Petr Fischl (born September 9, 1929), who perished in Oswiecim in 1944.

IT ALL DEPENDS ON HOW YOU LOOK AT IT

I.

Terezín is full of beauty.
It's in your eyes now clear
And through the street the tramp
Of many marching feet I hear.

In the ghetto at Terezín,
It looks that way to me,
Is a square kilometer of earth
Cut off from the world that's free.

II.

Death, after all, claims everyone,
You find it everywhere.
It catches up with even those
Who wear their noses in the air.

The whole, wide world is ruled
With a certain justice, so
That helps perhaps to sweeten
The poor man's pain and woe.

Miroslav Košek

MAN PROPOSES, GOD DISPOSES

I.

Who was helpless back in Prague,
And who was rich before,
He's a poor soul here in Terezín,
His body's bruised and sore.

II.

Who was toughened up before,
He'll survive these days.
But who was used to servants
Will sink into his grave.

Koleba (Miroslav Košek, Hanuš Löwy, Bachner)
26. II. 1944

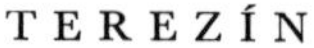

TEREZÍN

The heaviest wheel rolls across our foreheads
To bury itself deep somewhere inside our memories.

We've suffered here more than enough,
Here in this clot of grief and shame,
Wanting a badge of blindness
To be a proof for their own children.

A fourth year of waiting, like standing above a swamp
From which any moment might gush forth a spring.

Meanwhile, the rivers flow another way,
Another way,
Not letting you die, not letting you live.

And the cannons don't scream and the guns don't bark
And you don't see blood here.
Nothing, only silent hunger.
Children steal the bread here and ask and ask
                    and ask
And all would wish to sleep, keep silent and
      just to go to sleep again . . .

The heaviest wheel rolls across our foreheads
To bury itself deep somewhere inside our memories.

Mif 1944

TEREZÍN

That bit of filth in dirty walls,
And all around barbed wire,
And 30,000 souls who sleep
Who once will wake
And once will see
Their own blood spilled.

I was once a little child,
Three years ago.
That child who longed for other worlds.
But now I am no more a child
For I have learned to hate.
I am a grown-up person now,
I have known fear.

Bloody words and a dead day then,
That's something different than bogie men!

But anyway, I still believe I only sleep today,
That I'll wake up, a child again, and start to laugh and play.
I'll go back to childhood sweet like a briar rose,
Like a bell which wakes us from a dream,
Like a mother with an ailing child
Loves him with aching woman's love.
How tragic, then, is youth which lives
With enemies, with gallows ropes,
How tragic, then, for children on your lap
To say: this for the good, that for the bad.

Somewhere, far away out there, childhood sweetly sleeps,
Along that path among the trees,
There o'er that house
Which was once my pride and joy.
There my mother gave me birth into this world
So I could weep . . .

In the flame of candles by my bed, I sleep
And once perhaps I'll understand
That I was such a little thing,
As little as this song.

These 30,000 souls who sleep
Among the trees will wake,
Open an eye
And because they see
A lot

They'll fall asleep again . . .

Hanuš Hachenburg
IX. 1944

YES, THAT'S THE WAY THINGS ARE

I.

In Terezín in the so-called park
A queer old granddad sits
Somewhere there in the so-called park.
He wears a beard down to his lap
And on his head, a little cap.

II.

Hard crusts he crumbles in his gums,
He's only got one single tooth.
My poor old man with working gums,
Instead of soft rolls, lentil soup.
My poor old grey-beard!

Koleba (M. Košek, H. Löwy, Bachner)

14
15
16

PAIN STRIKES SPARKS ON ME, THE PAIN OF TEREZÍN

Fifteen beds. Fifteen charts with names,
Fifteen people without a family tree.
Fifteen bodies for whom torture is medicine and pills,
Beds over which the crimson blood of ages spills.
Fifteen bodies which want to live here.
Thirty eyes, seeking quietness.
Bald heads which gape from out the prison.
The holiness of the suffering, which is none of my business.

The loveliness of air, which day after day
Smells of strangeness and carbolic,
The nurses which carry thermometers
Mothers who grope after a smile.
Food is such a luxury here.
A long, long night, and a brief day.

But anyway, I don't want to leave
The lighted rooms and the burning cheeks,
Nurses who leave behind them only a shadow
To help the little sufferers.

I'd like to stay here, a small patient,
Waiting the doctor's daily round,
Until, after a long, long time, I'd be well again.

Then I'd like to live
And go back home again.

Anonymous

CONCERT IN THE OLD SCHOOL GARRET
(played by Gideon Klein)

White fingers of the sexton sleep heavy upon us.
Half a century
Since anyone as much as touched this piano.
Let it sing again
As it was made to yesterday.

Phantom hands which strike softly or which thunder.
The forehead of this man heavy as the
heavens before it rains.

And the springs,
Under the weight of excitement, forgot to squeak.
Half a century it is since anyone as much as touched
this piano.

Our good friend, Time,
Sucked each figure empty like a honeybee
Which has lived long enough
And drunk enough honey
So that now it can dry out in the sun somewhere.

Under the closed eyes, another person sits,
Under the closed eyes, he seeks among the keys
As among the veins through which the blood flows
softly
When you kiss them with a knife and put a song to it.

And this man yesterday cut all the veins,
Opening all the organ's stops,
Paid all the birds to sing,
To sing

Even though the harsh fingers of the sexton
sleep heavy upon us.
Bent in his manner of death, you are like Beethoven

Your forehead was as heavy as the heavens before it
rains.

Anonymous

THE BUTTERFLY

The last, the very last,
So richly, brightly, dazzlingly yellow.
Perhaps if the sun's tears would sing
against a white stone . . .

Such, such a yellow
Is carried lightly 'way up high.
It went away I'm sure because it wished to
kiss the world goodbye.

For seven weeks I've lived in here,
Penned up inside this ghetto
But I have found my people here.
The dandelions call to me
And the white chestnut candles in the court.
Only I never saw another butterfly.

That butterfly was the last one.
Butterflies don't live in here,
In the ghetto.

4. 6. 1942 Pavel Friedmann

THE LITTLE MOUSE

A mousie sat upon a shelf,
Catching fleas in his coat of fur.
But he couldn't catch her — what chagrin! —
She'd hidden 'way inside his skin.
He turned and wriggled, knew no rest,
That flea was such a nasty pest!

His daddy came
And searched his coat.
He caught the flea and off he ran
To cook her in the frying pan.
The little mouse cried, "Come and see!
For lunch we've got a nice, fat flea!"

26. II. 1944 Koleba (M. Košek, H. Löwy, Bachner)

HOMESICK

I've lived in the ghetto here more than a year,
In Terezín, in the black town now,
And when I remember my old home so dear,
I can love it more than I did, somehow.

Ah, home, home,
Why did they tear me away?
Here the weak die easy as a feather
And when they die, they die forever.

I'd like to go back home again,
It makes me think of sweet spring flowers.
Before, when I used to live at home,
It never seemed so dear and fair.

I remember now those golden days . . .
But maybe I'll be going there soon again.

People walk along the street,
You see at once on each you meet
That there's a ghetto here,
A place of evil and of fear.
There's little to eat and much to want,
Where bit by bit, it's horror to live.
But no one must give up!
The world turns and times change.

Yet we all hope the time will come
When we'll go home again.
Now I know how dear it is
And often I remember it.

9. III. 1943 ***Anonymous***

I'D LIKE TO GO ALONE

I'd like to go away alone
Where there are other, nicer people,
Somewhere into the far unknown,
There, where no one kills another.

Maybe more of us,
A thousand strong,
Will reach this goal
Before too long.

Alena Synková

Nina

5. VI. 1944

NIGHT IN THE GHETTO

Another day has gone for keeps
Into the bottomless pit of time.
Again it has wounded a man, held captive
    by his brethren.
After dusk, he longs for bandages,
For soft hands to shield the eyes
From all the horrors that stare by day.
But in the ghetto, darkness too is kind
To weary eyes which all day long
    Have had to watch.

Dawn crawls again along the ghetto streets
Embracing all who walk this way.
Only a car like a greeting from a long-gone world
Gobbles up the dark with fiery eyes —
That sweet darkness that falls upon the soul
And heals those wounds illumined by the day . . .
Along the streets come light and ranks of people
Like a long black ribbon, loomed with gold.

1943 Anonymous

FEAR

Today the ghetto knows a different fear,
Close in its grip, Death wields an icy scythe.
An evil sickness spreads a terror in its wake,
The victims of its shadow weep and writhe.

Today a father's heartbeat tells his fright
And mothers bend their heads into their hands.
Now children choke and die with typhus here,
A bitter tax is taken from their bands.

My heart still beats inside my breast
While friends depart for other worlds.
Perhaps it's better — who can say? —
Than watching this, to die today?

No, no, my God, we want to live!
Not watch our numbers melt away.
We want to have a better world,
We want to work — we must not die!

Eva Picková, 12 years old, Nymburk

TO OLGA

Listen!
The boat whistle has sounded now
And we must sail
Out toward an unknown port.

We'll sail a long, long way
And dreams will turn to truth.
Oh, how sweet the name Morocco!
Listen!
Now it's time.

The wind sings songs of far away,
Just look up to heaven
And think about the violets.

Listen!
Now it's time.

Alena Synková

FORGOTTEN

You wanton, quiet memory that haunts me all the while
In order to remind me of her whom love I send.
Perhaps when you caress me sweetly, I will smile,
You are my confidante today, my very dearest friend.

You sweet remembrance, tell a fairy tale
About my girl who's lost and gone, you see.
Tell, tell the one about the golden grail
And call the swallow, bring her back to me.

Fly somewhere back to her and ask her, soft and low,
If she thinks of me sometimes with love,
If she is well and ask her too before you go
If I am still her dearest, precious dove.

And hurry back, don't lose your way,
So I can think of other things,
But you were too lovely, perhaps, to stay.
I loved you once. Goodbye, my love!

Anonymous

THE GARDEN

A little garden,
Fragrant and full of roses.
The path is narrow
And a little boy walks along it.

A little boy, a sweet boy,
Like that growing blossom.
When the blossom comes to bloom,
The little boy will be no more.

Franta Bass

ON A SUNNY EVENING

On a purple, sun-shot evening
Under wide-flowering chestnut trees
Upon the threshold full of dust
Yesterday, today, the days are all like these.

Trees flower forth in beauty,
Lovely too their very wood all gnarled and old
That I am half afraid to peer
Into their crowns of green and gold.

The sun has made a veil of gold
So lovely that my body aches.
Above, the heavens shriek with blue
Convinced I've smiled by some mistake.
The world's abloom and seems to smile.
I want to fly but where, how high?
If in barbed wire, things can bloom
Why couldn't I? I will not die!

1944 Anonymous
Written by the children in Barracks L 318 and L 417,
ages 10—16 years.

BIRDSONG

He doesn't know the world at all
Who stays in his nest and doesn't go out.
He doesn't know what birds know best
Nor what I want to sing about,
That the world is full of loveliness.

When dewdrops sparkle in the grass
And earth's aflood with morning light,
A blackbird sings upon a bush
To greet the dawning after night.
Then I know how fine it is to live.

Hey, try to open up your heart
To beauty; go to the woods someday
And weave a wreath of memory there.
Then if the tears obscure your way
You'll know how wonderful it is
　　To be alive.

1941 Anonymous

The poor thing stands there vainly,
Vainly he strains his voice.
Perhaps he'll die. Than can you say
How beautiful is the world today?

Anonymous

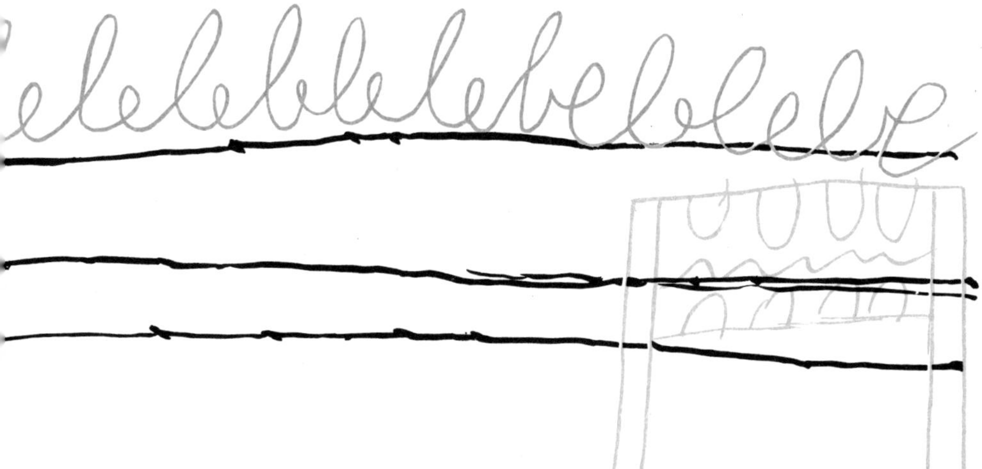

EPILOGUE

A FEW WORDS ABOUT THIS BOOK

In Czechoslovakia, there is a strange place called Terezín, some 60 kilometers from Prague. It was founded by order of Emperor Joseph II of Austria, 200 years ago and named after his mother, Maria Theresa. This walled-in fortress was constructed on plans drafted by Italian military engineers and has 12 ramparts which enclose the town in the shape of a star. It was to have been a fortress and it became a sleepy army garrison dominated by the barracks, where the homes of the inhabitants were a necessary nuisance. There were homes, taverns, a post office, a bank and a brewery. There was a church as well, built in a sober style and belonging to the barracks as part of the army community. The little town seemed to have been forced onto the countryside, a lovely countryside without either high mountains or dizzy cliffs, without deep ravines or swift rivers... only blue hills, green meadows, fruit trees, and tall poplars.

Today, a shadow still lingers above this little town as though funeral wagons still drive along its streets, as though the dust still eddies in the town square, stirred by a thousand footsteps. Today, it seems sometimes as though from every corner, from every stairway and from every corridor, peer human faces, gaunt, exhausted, with eyes full of fear.

During the war years, Terezín was a place of famine and of fear. Somewhere far away, in Berlin, men in uniforms had held meetings. These men decided to exterminate all the Jews in Europe, and because they were used to doing things thoroughly with the calculated, cool passion of a murderer, they worked out plans in which they fixed the country, the place and the timetable as well as the stopping-places on that road to death. One of these stopping places was Terezín.

It was meant to be a model camp which foreigners could be shown, and it was termed a ghetto. At first, Jews from Bohemia and Moravia were brought to Terezín, but finally they came from all over Europe and from hence were shipped further east to the gas chambers and ovens. Everything in this small town was false, invented; every one of its inhabitants was condemned in advance to die. It was only a funnel without an outlet. Those who contrived this trap and put it on their map, with its fixed timetable of life and death, knew all about it. They knew its future as well. Those who were brought here in crowded railroad coaches and cattle cars after days and days of cruelty, of humiliation, of offense, of beatings and of theft, knew very little about it. Some of them believed the murderers' falsehoods, that they could sit out the war here in quiet safety. Others came to Terezín already crushed, yet with a spark of hope that even so, perhaps they might escape their destiny. There were also those who knew that Terezín was only one station on a short timetable and that is why they tried so hard to keep at least themselves alive and perhaps their family. And those who were good and honorable, endeavored to keep the children alive, the aged and the ailing. All were finally deceived and the same fate awaited all of them.

But the children who were brought here knew nothing. They came from places where they had already known humiliation; they had been expelled from the schools. They had sewn stars on their hearts, on their jackets and blouses, and were only allowed to play in the cemeteries. That wasn't so bad, if you look at it with the eyes of a child, even when they heard their parents' lamentations, even when they heard strange words charged with horror such as mapping, registration and transport. When they were herded with their parents into the ghetto, when they had to sleep on the concrete floors in crowded garrets or clamber up three-tiered bunks, they began to look around and quickly understood the strange world in which they had to live. They saw reality, but they still maintained their childish outlook, an outlook of truth which distinguishes between night and day and cannot be confused with false hopes and the shadowplay of an imaginary life.

And so they lived, locked within walls and courtyards. This was their world, a world of color and shadow, of hunger and of hope.

The children played in the barracks yard and the courtyards of the one-time homes. Sometimes they were permitted to breathe a little fresh air upon the ramparts. From the age of 14, they had to work, to live the life of an adult. Sometimes they went beyond the walls to work in the gardens and they were no more considered to be children. The smaller ones acted out their fairy tales and even children's operas. But they did not know that they too, as well as the grown-ups, had been used deceitfully, in an effort to convince a commission of foreigners from the Red Cross that Terezín was a place where adults and children alike could live. Secretly, they studied and they drew pictures. Three months, half a year, one or two years, depending on one's luck, because transports came and went continually, headed east into nothingness.

From these 15,000 children, which for a time played and drew pictures and studied, only 100 came back. They saw everything that grown-ups saw. They saw the endless queues in front of the canteens, they saw the funeral carts used to carry bread and the human beings harnessed to pull them. They saw the infirmaries which seemed like a paradise to them and funerals which were only a gathering-up of coffins. They saw executions too and were perhaps the only children in the world who captured them with pencil and paper.

They listened to a speech made up of a hodgepodge of expressions like bonke, shlajska, shahojista, and they learned to speak this language. They heard the shouts of the SS-men at roll call and the meek mumblings of prayer in the barracks where the grown-ups lived.

But the children saw too what the grown-ups didn't want to see—the beauties beyond the village gates, the green meadows and the bluish hills, the ribbon of highway reaching off into the distance and the imagined road marker pointing toward Prague, the animals, the birds, the butterflies—all this was beyond the village walls and they could look at it only from afar, from the barracks windows and from the ramparts of the fort. They saw things too that grown-ups cannot see—princesses with coronets, evil wizards and witches, jesters and bugs with human faces, a land of happiness where for an admission of one crown, there was everything to be had—cookies, candy, a roast pig stuck with a fork from which milk and sodapop trickled. They saw too the rooms they'd lived in at home, with curtains at the window and a kitten and a saucer of milk. But they transported it to Terezín. There had to be a fence and a lot of pots and pans, because there was supposed to be food in every pot and pan.

All this they drew and painted and many other things besides; they loved to paint and draw, from morning till evening.

But when they wrote poems, it was something else again. Here one finds words about "painful Terezín", about "the little girl who got lost". These told of longings to go away somewhere where there are kinder people; there are old grandfathers gnawing stale bread and rotten potatoes for lunch, there was a "longing for home" and fear. Yes, fear came to them and they could tell of it in their poems, knowing that they were condemned. Perhaps they knew it better than the adults.

There were 15,000 of them and 100 came back. You are looking at their drawings now after many years, when that world of hunger, fear and horror seems to us almost like a cruel fairy tale about evil wizards, witches and cannibals. The drawings and poems—that is all that is left of these children, for their ashes have long since sifted across the fields around Oswiecim. Their signatures are here and some of the drawings are inscribed with the year, and the number of their group. Of those who signed their names, it has been possible to find out a few facts: the year and place of their birth, the number of their transport to Terezín and to Oswiecim and then the year of their death. For most of them, it was 1944, the next to last year of World War II.

But their drawings and their poems speak to us; these are their voices which have been preserved, voices of reminder, of truth and of hope.

We are publishing them not as dry documents out of thousands such witnesses in a sea of suffering, but in order to honor the memory of those who created these colors and these words. That's the way these children probably would have wanted it when death overtook them.

JIŘÍ WEIL

CATALOG OF DRAWINGS

The children's drawings from Terezín collected in this publication have been chosen from a total of 4,000 drawings in the archives of the State Jewish Museum in Prague. They were given to the Museum during the post-war collection of documents on the persecution at Terezín. The drawings were given in envelopes bearing the number of different "homes" (for instance C III, B IV, 1 417 etc.) where the children lived at Terezín and where they were secretly given schooling.

To illustrate this publication, two kinds of drawings were chosen: some as illustrations of the poems' texts, others for their artistic value. A total of 39 children are represented in the illustrations. The dates of their birth and death are listed in the index of drawings. From indications on the drawings themselves and a comparison of the children's biographical material, it has been established that the earliest drawing dates from 1943, although it is known that the children were drawing pictures as soon as they came to Terezín.

Children were consciously guided to drawing, as is indicated by the notes of their instructors who taught in the girls' and boys' dormitories. The teaching program was carefully planned and classes were divided into several levels. They began with the required fundamentals of drawing (wavy lines, circles) and later the children drew pictures of everyday objects which they saw around them at Terezín such as jelly jars filled with meadow flowers and finally, complicated still lifes, drawn from nature.

Because the instructors were not trained teachers and permitted the children to draw whatever they wanted to, even to copy from reproductions of famous masterpieces which happened to be at hand (Cranach, Titian, Cézanne, Van Gogh, Matisse), scores of accurate copies were preserved as well as drawings which were only indirectly inspired by modern art. We find many drawings which are reminiscent of modern Czech painters such as Václav Špála and Emil Filla, whose works were certainly familiar to some of the children.

From the artistic standpoint, the most interesting are first of all the collages, made out of all sorts of materials which happened to be around, such as old office forms, wrapping paper etc. and which were cut or torn into various shapes and designs. These designs pasted on paper reflect in their composition and color combinations the artistic trends at the beginning of the 20th century.

The great majority of the drawings date from the first half of 1944. Fewer are found from the autumn of 1944, when the steady shipment of Terezín prisoners eastward interrupted the school program and when the majority of the children, together with their drawing teacher, F. Brandejsova, left Terezín.

Out of the whole collection of drawings, it is possible to distinguish the work of boys and girls. They differ not only in other interests, but also in their approach to assigned or individually chosen themes. Girls were more interested in nature which they remembered; they paid more attention to flowers, to butterflies: they drew ballerinas, pretty little cottages with flower gardens and so on. Boys were much more concrete. They were interested in the details of the hilly landscape of the Czech Central Mountains and the Ohře River, which flows among these once-volcanic hills and which they decked with steamboats, warships etc. They busied themselves illustrating detective stories and we find an entire cycle of drawing of battles, revelries and other adventures. Just as concretely did they draw pictures of everyday life at Terezín and of its inhabitants. They made pictures of SS men, ghetto guards, of carts drawn by human beings, of burials or executions. These drawings of course were done outside of the school program, since those made as part of the regular instruction can be identified by theme. All the drawings which have been preserved, whether their theme was suggested by the teacher or chosen freely by the children themselves, are individual creations. The children were not encumbered by formal school patterns and that is why we find such great appeal in these children's artistic expressions.

Page 3 MAN HOLDING NEWSPAPER WITH AN INCORRECTLY WRITTEN INSCRIPTION, TAGESBEHFEL (official Terezín bulletin).

The detail of the upper right part of the drawing, "Scenes from Life at Terezín", a drawing on both sides of the paper, done in pencil and pastel crayon on semi-glossy yellow paper (archives number 129.075, 20.3 × 29 cm, 1942—1945 written in later). On the other side of the drawing "Zuzka Winterová Block IV 4/8" is written in the upper right corner.

Zuzana Winterová was born January 27, 1933, in Brno, and deported to Terezín on April 4, 1942. She is represented in the collection of children's drawings from Terezín by another pastel, "Mommy with a Baby Carriage", dated April 11, 1944, and the sketch, "Elephant", from April 18, 1944, which was a common assignment for children in her age group who were living in Block IV. She perished in Oswiecim on October 4, 1944.

Page 5 BUTTERFLIES

A pencil drawing on the back of a double sheet of glossy yellow paper (archives number 129.498, 20.5 × 28.9 cm). On the front, "Eva Bu" (Bulová) is written in the upper right corner.

Eva Bulová was born July 12, 1930, at Řevnice near Prague and brought to Terezín on September 12, 1942. She is represented by 11 other drawings in this collection, the most interesting of which artistically is the collage, "Portrait of a Woman with Long Hair". At Terezín, Eva lived in house number 28 and was put into Group A. She died October 4, 1944, in Oswiecim.

Page 6 SKETCH OF CHILDREN'S HANDS

The reverse side of a pencil sketch (archives number 129.411, 20.5 × 16 m). In the lower right corner of the other side is written "František Brozan L 417 Heim X 2".

František Brozan was born on December 13, 1932, in Staňkov and deported to Terezín on November 30, 1942. He is represented in this collection by two more drawings: a pencil sketch, "Tools", which was an assignment for children of his age, and a watercolor, "Landscape". He lived in house number 10 at Terezín and died at Oswiecim on December 15, 1943.

Page 9 CHILDREN HOLDING HANDS

A detail from the lower right part of a sketch, "Children in the Park", done in pencil on tinted paper (archives number 129.950, 22 × 32 cm). The upper left corner is marked "G. Frei (I) XIII III 11 Jahre".

Gabriela Freiová was born on January 1, 1933, in Holice in Bohemia and was deported to Terezín on December 9, 1942. She is represented in the collection by 24 other drawings, most of them done with colored pencils. One, an exception, is dated 1943 (Ship at Sea), while the others were made between January and May, 1944. At Terezín, she lived in house number 13 and was in the III school group. The last drawing, "Tightrope Walker", is dated May 10, 1944. She died eight days later in Oswiecim.

Page 10 FIGURE OF A GIRL

A detail of the upper left corner of a sketch of human figures done in pencil on both sides of tinted paper (archives number 125.423, 17.5 × 23 cm). In the upper left corner, there is the inscription "Marion Mayer, 9 Jahre, 7. Stunde, C III 104"

She was born in 1935. The date of her arrival in Terezín and the date of her death is not known. She is represented in the collection with another watercolor, "Stadium" and with a drawing done with colored pencils, "Animals", which was the theme assigned to children in the 8th class. The drawings show that she was nine years old and lived in house C III 104.

Page 11 TEREZÍN BARRACKS

Detail of a watercolor on tinted paper (archives number 129.361, 22 × 30 cm); reduced by one third. The left corner is inscribed "Sonja W. 16" (Waldsteinová) in the handwriting of the teacher, F. Brandejsová.

Sonja Waldsteinová was born in Prague on November 28, 1926, and was deported to Terezín on March 6, 1943. She is represented in this collection with four more drawings which differ in character from the rest of the art work from Terezín. Hers are mature sketches, the work of a trained and talented pupil who did not limit herself to school assignment. Sonja Waldsteinová returned to Prague after the liberation.

Page 12 WINDOW WITH BARS

A detail of the middle portion of a drawing by the same name. It covers both sides of a grey paper and is done with pastels (archives number 129.459, 20 × 31 cm). On the left side is written "Erika Taussig IV h 28.6. 44".

Erika Taussigová was born in Prague on October 28, 1934, and was deported to Terezín on December 17, 1941. She is represented in this collection with 15 other drawings, most of them pastels and watercolors, dated between April and June, 1944. From her drawings, with their careful inscriptions, we learn that Erika lived in house number C III and later in Block IV. One of the most interesting of her drawings is "Heart with a Horseshoe", dedicated to her teacher with the inscription, "Fir frau Brandajs-Erika", dated April 8, 1944. She died at Oswiecim on October 16, 1944.

Page 13 MEN WITH STRETCHER

Detail from lower portion of drawing, "Impressions from Life at Terezín". It is done in pencil on the back of a piece of glossy red paper (archives number 129.408, 24.3 × 25.2 cm; enlarged by half). In the upper right corner is written "Weisskopf S VII X".

Alfred Weisskopf was born on January 24, 1932, in Prague and deported to Terezín on December 22, 1942. He has six more drawings among this collection of children's art from Terezín, and these are among the most interesting because they take their themes from Terezín itself and its environs. He lived in building L 417, house number X. Perished December 18, 1944, in Oswiecim.

Page 14 QUEUE FOR FOOD

Detail from upper right part of drawing, "Serving Meals". It covers both sides of a piece of wrapping paper and is drawn in pencil (archives number 129.204, 22 × 30 cm; the illustration is enlarged to twice its original size by mirror reproduction). Written on the reverse is "Liana Franklová HOD. 13, DOMOV 13."

Liana Franklová was born in Brno on January 12, 1931, and deported to Terezín on December 5, 1941. Another 19 of her drawings are included in the collection, most of them pastels and watercolors, dating between March and May, 1944. In Terezín, she lived in house 13 and belonged to group IV. One of her most interesting works is a pencil sketch, "The Tree of Happiness", which reflects the wishes of all the children at Terezín—platters of food, roast chicken, fruit, vegetables etc. Died in Oswiecim on October 19, 1944.

Page 15 COOK SERVING FOOD

Detail from drawing by Liana Franklová (see page 14). Enlarged by two and a half times its original size. Mirror reproduction.

Page 16 VIEW OF TEREZÍN

Detail of central part of paper cut-out collage (archives number 131.236, 21 × 32 cm). On the other side of the paper is written, "Hans Weinberg HEIM II stunde 6".

Hanuš Weinberg was born in Ústí nad Orlicí on August 18, 1931, and deported to Terezín on December 5, 1942. Two more of his watercolors and two pencil sketches, their themes suggested by his teacher, are included in this collection. In Terezín, he lived in boys' dormitory number II. Perished in Oswiecim on December 15, 1943.

Page 17 FIGURE OF SS MAN

Detail from central portion of drawing, "People of Terezín". A pencil sketch done on both sides of a piece of blotting paper (archives number 125.426, 22.2 × 28.7 cm). Written in upper left corner: "BEUTLER JIŘÍ L 417/7".

Jiří Beutler was born March 9, 1932, in Frýdlant nad Ostravicí and deported to Terezín on September 18, 1942. He has 13 other drawings in this collection, most of them watercolors and pasted cut-outs. He lived in building L 417, houses X and 7, while in Terezín. Perished at Oswiecim on May, 18, 1944.

Page 18 CARICATURE OF FIGURE WITH BANDAGE

Detail from left center part of sketch, "The Ailing". It is a pencil drawing on tinted paper (archives number 129.205, 23.7 × 23 cm). No signature. Four and a half times enlarged.

Page 19 CARICATURE OF A MAN

Detail from drawing (page 18). Four times enlarged.

Page 20 FIGURES OF LITTLE GIRLS

Right half of drawing by same name. It is a pencil sketch done on writing paper (archives number 129.412. 14.6×22.2 cm: enlarged to twice its size). On left corner it is signed "JANA HELLEROVÁ 6 Roku, C III 1 h".

Jana Hellerová was born on February 3, 1938, in Prague and deported to Terezín on July 15, 1943. She was the youngest pupil in the Terezín "school". She has one other pencil drawing among the collection, also from the first class. Died October 16, 1944, at Oswiecim.

Page 21 CZECH CENTRAL MOUNTAINS LANDSCAPE

Right part of pasted paper cut-outs on tinted paper (archives number 129.737, 20.2 × 32 cm). It is signed "3 Stunde Eva Stein L 318" in the lower right corner.

Eva Steinová was born in Prague on September 4, 1931, and deported to Terezín on December 14, 1941. She has 15 more drawings included in this collection, most of them pencil sketches. At Terezín, she lived in building L 318, house number 14 and at the end, in house L 410, and was a member of the II group. Three of her drawings are dated May 1944; a sketchbook with six pages dates from the fall of 1944 and, according to the general school custom, inscribed 1944—45. She died at Oswiecim on October 23, 1944.

Page 23 LEAVES OF A TREE

Detail from lower right portion of drawing, "Study of Leaves", a black watercolor done on tinted paper (archives number 131.120, 21.7×34 cm). Signed on upper right corner, "Biennenfeld Milan Heim II".

Milan Biennenfeld was born in Prague on March 28, 1930, and deported to Terezín on October 24, 1942. He has one more pencil sketch included in the collection of children's art from Terezín, where he was a member of the 10th class. He lived in boys' dormitory II at Terezín. Died May 18, 1944, at Oswiecim.

Pages 24 and 25 GARDEN

Watercolor on tinted paper (archives number 129.394, 16.5×25.2 cm; one and a half times enlarged). It is signed "I. Ruth Čech" in the lower right corner.

Ruth Čechová was born in Brno on April 19, 1931, and brought to Terezín on March 19, 1943. She has 13 more drawings, pastels, watercolors and pencil sketches included in this collection, most of which are dated between April and June, 1944. At Terezín, Ruth lived in house number C III and was a member of group I. Died at Oswiecim on October 19, 1944.

Pages 26 and 27 MEADOW FLOWERS

Pencil drawing on both sides of a piece of tinted paper (archives number 125.508, 26.2×21.3 cm; page 27, mirror reproduction). The reverse side is signed "Hanuš Weinberg HEIM II s 7" in the upper right corner.

Biographical material about Hanuš Weinberg is found on page 67.

Page 27 MAN WITH A LONG BEARD

Pencil drawing on tinted paper (archives number 129.774, 20.3 × 21.5 cm). Signed "MEITNER EVA" in lower left corner.
Eva Meitnerová was born in Prostějov on May 1, 1931, and deported to Terezín on July 4, 1942. Another 22 of her drawings, mainly pencil sketches and pastels, are included in this collection. One of the most interesting is the pastel, "Seder", depicting a holiday supper during Passover in which the children had participated in their homes. In Terezín, she lived in house number 14 and belonged to group IV.
Died October 28, 1944, in Oswiecim.

Pages 28 and 29 DWELLINGS IN TEREZÍN

Detail from a watercolor, reduced in size on the right side by one third. It is on tinted paper (archives number 129.406, 14.7 × 21 cm; twice enlarged). On the upper right corner it is signed "Hana Grünfeld. VI. 1944 4B". Hana Grünfeldová was born on May 20, 1935, place unknown, and deported to Terezín on December 14, 1941. She has nine more drawings included in this collection, most of them dating between April and June, 1944. She lived in Block IV at Terezín and perished at Oswiecim in 1944.

Page 30 FIGURE OF A BOY

Detail from a drawing by Marion Mayerová (see page 10). Enlarged two and a half times.

Page 31 FANTASY

Pasted paper collage on office form (archives number 129.466, 20.3 × 25.3 cm; reproduced vertically). Signed "Lissauová Hana heim 28 5 2. III" on reverse side.
Hana Lissauová was born February 4, 1930, in Lány and deported to Terezín on February 25, 1942. She has 22 additional drawings in the collection, mostly pencil sketches based on themes suggested by her teacher. Two drawings date from February and May, 1944. She lived in house number 28 at Terezín and belonged to group A. Perished at Oswiecim on October 16, 1944.

Page 32 BUTTERFLIES

Detail from middle part of a watercolor painted on the reverse side of a piece of glossy yellow paper (archives number 129.498, 20.5 × 28.9 cm; enlarged by one third). Signed "Eva Bu" (Bulová) in upper right corner. For biographical data, see page 65.

Page 33 IRIS

Detail from a watercolor and pencil sketch done on both sides of a piece of drawing paper (archives number 129. 940, 19.8 × 27.6 cm; for this illustration, the left part of the drawing is used). Signed "4 h Erika Taussig". Biographical data on page 66.

Page 34 DANCING CHILDREN

Watercolor on grey paper (archives number 129.963, 21.7 × 32 cm). Signed on right side: "Helena Schanzerová 2 skupina 2 III".

Helena Schanzerová was born in Prague on November 3, 1933, and deported to Terezín on July 30, 1942. She has six more drawings included in this collection. At Terezín, Helena lived in building C III, house number 13 and belonged to Group I. Died May 18, 1944, in Oswiecim.

Page 35 See drawing on page 34. Mirror reproduction.

Page 35 THE MOUSE

Detail from the lower right corner of drawing, "Domestic Animals". An anonymous pastel sketch on the reverse side of a piece of shiny green paper (archives number 121.501, 19.8 × 25 cm). Signed "XIII" in lower right corner.

Pages 36 and 37 HOUSE

Detail from pasted collage on office form (archives number 129.715, 14.8 × 21 cm, left side diminished by one fourth, mirror reproduction, enlarged by half). Signature on reverse side: "Valentíková Dita I. s".

Dita Valentíková was born in 1933, but nothing more is known about her. There are 15 more drawings by her in the collection, dated from May and June, 1944. In Terezín she lived in building L 410, house 16, and in building C III. She belonged to Group I.

Pages 38 and 39 GIRL LOOKING OUT OF THE WINDOW

Watercolor on tinted paper (archives number 129.389, 21 × 25.8 cm). Signature on reverse side: "Nina Ledererová I III".

Nina Ledererová was born September 7, 1931, in Prague and deported to Terezín on September 8, 1942. She has nine other drawings among the collection of children's art from Terezín, most of which were based on assigned themes. They date from April to May, 1944. She was a member of Group II. Her last drawings, "Flower Study" and "Sketch", were done on May 9, 1944. Died in Oswiecim on May 15, 1944.

Pages 40 and 41 FANTASY

Watercolor on the grey cover of a sketchbook (archives number 125.420, 13.6 × 21 cm, twice enlarged for this illustration). Signed "SILVÍN VI. 25. VI. 1944" at bottom.

Nely Silvínová was born in Prague on December 21, 1931, and deported to Terezín on August 10, 1942. Sixteen more of her drawings are included in this collection, all of which have interesting color compositions. Most of them date between April and June, 1944. At Terezín, she lived in house number 14 and belonged to Group V. Died October 4, 1944, in Oswiecim.

Page 42 CANDLESTICK

Detail from middle part of drawing, "Interior". It is done in pastels on the reverse side of a piece of semi-glossy yellow paper (archives number 129.209, 17.5 × 25 cm). On the upper left corner is inscribed "Karpeles Ireni".

Irena Karpelesová was born in Prague on December 30, 1930, and deported to Terezín on December 22, 1942. She has 27 other drawings included in this collection, their themes suggested either by her teacher or chosen by herself and reflecting life in Terezín and its environs. At Terezín, Irena lived in house number 13 and belonged to Group A. Died October 23, 1944, in Oswiecim.

Page 43 DWELLINGS IN TEREZÍN

Left half of a pencil drawing done on grey cardboard (archives number 129.407, 19 × 24 cm; enlarged by one third). Signature on back of drawing: "NOVÁK J. X 1943 13 stunde".

Josef Novák was born on October 25, 1931, in Prague and deported to Terezín on April 24, 1942. Another 16 sketches, watercolors and pencil drawings have been preserved in the collection of children's art from Terezín. The subject matter of the drawings dated 1943 have a patriotic inspiration (Flowering of the Czech Nation, For the Nation), but there is also a picture of a Terezín execution (January 1, 1942), made from a description which he had heard. He lived in the boys' dormitory X in Terezín and died May 18, 1944, in Oswiecim.

Page 44 FANTASY

The detail from middle portion of a pencil sketch on tinted paper (archives number 125.433, 22 × 28.6 cm, enlarged by one fourth). On the lower right corner there is a notation in the handwriting of teacher F. Brandejsová, "Raja 25" (Engländerová).

Raja Engländerová was born in Prague on August 25, 1929, and deported to Terezín on January 30, 1942. The collection of children's art from Terezín contains 23 more of her drawings, mostly watercolors and pencil sketches. She was among the talented pupils, drawing mainly from her own chosen themes. Part of the drawings are dated from April to May, 1944. In Terezín she lived in house number 25. After the liberation, she returned to Prague.

Page 45 THE GHETTO GUARD

Detail from central part of drawing, "Impressions of Life at Terezín". A pencil sketch on two sides of the paper (archives number 129.355, 21 × 25.2 cm). The upper right corner is signed "V. Flusser 2 h[illegible]d X". Vladimír Flusser was born in Prague on March 12, 1931, and deported to Terezín on July 16, 1942. He lived in boys' dormitory X and died in Oswiecim on September 6, 1943.

Page 46 PALM TREE

Detail from middle portion of drawing, "Africa", a pencil and pastel sketch on the back of a sheet of semi-glossy yellow paper (archives number 125.405, 16.5 × 22.7 cm, colors added later). It is signed "Eva Heská IV sk" in the upperl left corner.

Eva Heská was born in Přerov on May 29, 1930, and deported to Terezín on June 26, 1942. In the collection of children's art from Terezín, another 19 of her drawings are found, dating from February to May, 1944. She lived in house number 13 at Terezín and belonged to group IV, being a diligent drawing pupil as is reflected in her drawing, "Paradise—Forbidden Fruit", from the 35th class period. Died May 18, 1944, in Oswiecim.

Page 47 MAN ON A BOAT

Detail from middle part of drawing by the same name, done in pastels on tinted paper (archives number 129.061, 16.7 × 21.5 cm; twice enlarged). Inscription in upper right: "Elly HELLER 28. III 1944".

Cover: CZECH CENTRAL MOUNTAINS LANDSCAPE
Right part of pasted paper cut-outs on tinted paper by Eva Steinová (archives number 129.737, 20.2 × 32 cm)

CATALOG OF POEMS

The originals of these poems by the children of Terezín are in the archives of the State Jewish Museum in Prague. They were turned over to the Museum on November 3, 1952, by Mrs. A. Flachová of Brno, and were part of the property of her husband who had been a teacher in one of the Terezín children's homes, L 417. There are 42 of these manuscripts and in typed copy, 24. The folio in which the poems were given, bears the following inscription: TEREZÍN 1941—1945, 1.) poems written by children from the children's homes (up to the age of 16), 2.) Ester particularly for Terezín (scratched out with an indelible pencil), 3.) poems about Terezín. The folio evidently dates from a later period. It contained those poems listed in the archives under the number 108.218. A copy of the poem, "Fear", by Eva Picková, was given to the State Jewish Museum in 1955 by Dr. R. Feder. The prose of Petr Fischl, "The Diary of Pavel Bondy", archives number 101.517/55, is deposited in the Museum archives in typed copy and was donated during the Museum's documentation campaign in 1945 when written records and memoirs from the former Terezín ghetto were collected.

The collection was made of artistic as well as documentary material.

The children at Terezín were consciously guided to literary expression; in one of the children's homes, poetry contests and recitation evenings of children's poems were held. The older children took an active part as reciters and actors in the extensive cultural programs which were arranged. During secret school instruction, as well as at lectures, they got acquainted with old and new literary works. The poems of the older children were influenced by the work of the younger generation of Czech poets and differ from the so-called Protectorate poetry of that time in that contemporary material predominates. There is no escape into general abstract themes; these poems represent a direct reaction to the surroundings in which they were written and they differ too in that they seek to express in the form of modern poetry the tragic fate of the prisoners of Terezín.

The poems by the younger children are in the form of nursery rhymes and were influenced by picture books and primers which were widely circulated in Terezín, printed on a hectograph. It is characteristic of these rhymes that they too deal with the themes of Terezín and that they, like the poems of the older children, reflect the life of Terezín in all its sufferings.

Page 9 THE BUTTERFLY

Quotation from Pavel Friedmann's poem, "The Butterfly". For further facts, see page 33.

Page 10 AT TEREZÍN

A children's rhyme written in pencil on a piece of drawing paper. The handwriting is simple, childish and there are no grammatical errors. It is signed "Teddy" in the right corner. "1943" and "L 410" have been added in another handwriting. The author's name cannot be determined, but he was probably a member of the same group as Miroslav Košek, with whom he lived in children's home L 410.

Page 13 THE CLOSED TOWN

The poem is preserved in a typewritten copy. All other facts are unknown.

Page 14 . . . WE GOT USED TO STANDING . . .

Excerpt from the prose of Petr Fischl "Diary of Pavel Bondy". The typed copy is written on a piece of thin copy paper and was donated to the State Jewish Museum during its documentation campaign.

Petr Fischl was born in Prague on September 9, 1929, and deported to Terezín on December 8, 1943. He died at Oswiecim on October 8, 1944. His work is lyrical prose, but his description of Terezín is exceptional for its accuracy and sober tone.

Page 17 IT ALL DEPENDS ON HOW YOU LOOK AT IT

A children's rhyme in two stanzas, written in pen on a German office form. There is the following signature in the upper left corner: "Mir. Košek". The poem is written in a child's script without grammatical errors. Miroslav Košek was born on March 30, 1932, at Hořelice in Bohemia and deported to Terezín on February 15, 1942. He died on October 19, 1944 at Oswiecim. At Terezín, he lived in children's home L 410.

Page 19 MAN PROPOSES, GOD DISPOSES

Children's rhyme written in pen on a German office form. It is signed "Koleba: Košek, Löwy, Bachner" in the upper right corner. In the left corner, "26/II" is written in a different script. The rhyme is in a childish handwriting with grammatical errors which have been corrected in pencil by someone else.

Miroslav Košek: for biographical data, see previous entry. No information about Bachner could be found. The third author, Hanuš Löwy, was born in Ostrava on June 29, 1931, and deported to Terezín on September 30, 1942. He died in Oswiecim on October 4, 1944.

Page 20 TEREZÍN

This poem is preserved in a typewritten copy. "1944" is written in pencil in the upper right corner. In the seventh line, the words "two years" have been altered in brown pencil to "four years". In the lower right corner is the pencil signature, "Mif".

Pages 22 and 23 TEREZÍN

The poem is preserved in a typewritten copy. In the right corner, "IX. 1944" is written in and on the right side, the following is written in pencil: "Written by children from the ages of 10 to 16, living in homes L 318 and L 417". The poem is unsigned. The author was identified by O. Klein, former teacher at Terezín, as Hanuš Hachenburg.

Hanuš Hachenburg was born in Prague on July 12, 1929, and deported to Terezín on October 24, 1942. He died on December 18, 1943, in Oswiecim. The copy probably is from a later date.

Page 26 YES, THAT'S THE WAY THINGS ARE

Children's rhyme in two stanzas written in pen on a German office form. The signature at the bottom reads "Koleba: Košek, Löwy, Bachner". It is written in a child's script without grammatical errors. For further data, see previous page.

Page 29 PAIN STRIKES SPARKS ON ME, THE PAIN OF TEREZÍN

This poem is preserved in manuscript form written in pen on a piece of paper torn out of a notebook. There are three other poems on this same sheet of paper, one of which is crossed out. From the letters it seems probable that it is copy. No biographical date is available.

Page 30 CONCERT IN THE OLD SCHOOL GARRET

The poem is preserved in typewritten copy. "Played by Gideon Klein" is written in pencil in the upper right corner. No other data.

Page 33 THE BUTTERFLY

The poem is preserved in typewritten copy on thin copy paper in the collection of poetry by Pavel Friedmann which was donated to the National Jewish Museum during its documentation campaign. (Archives number 101.516, 1–8). It is dated June 4, 1942, in the left corner.

Pavel Friedmann was born January 7, 1921, in Prague and deported to Terezín on April 26, 1942. He died in Oswiecim on September 29, 1944. Although in years he belongs among the adult poets, his work does not differ much in style or subject matter from the work of younger poets.

Pages 34 and 35 THE LITTLE MOUSE

A children's verse written in pen on a German office form, having two stanzas. "Koleba: Košek, Löwy, Bachner" is written in the right corner and above it in pencil, "26/II". The handwriting is that of a child and there are no grammatical errors. For further facts, see previous page.

Page 36 HOMESICK

The poem is preserved in manuscript, written in pencil on a sheet of lined paper torn from a notebook. The date "9. III. 1943" is in the upper right corner. All other facts missing.

Page 38 I'D LIKE TO GO ALONE

Preserved in manuscript, written in pencil on a scrap of yellowed paper. On the other side is the inscription "Alena Synková" in ink.

Alena Synková was born in Prague on September 24, 1926, and deported to Terezín on December 22, 1942. She returned home after the liberation.

Page 42 NIGHT IN THE GHETTO

The poem is preserved in manuscript, written in pen on a sheet of white paper, together with three more poems by the same author. At the bottom underneath the poem in the middle of the page is the date "1943" and on the other side, "L 410" written by a different hand in pencil. All other information lacking.

Page 45 FEAR

The poem is preserved in a copy turned over to the State Jewish Museum in Prague by Dr. R. Feder in 1955. It is signed at the bottom, "12 year old Eva Picková from Nymburk".

Eva Picková was born in Nymburk on May 15, 1929, deported to Terezín on April 16, 1942, and perished in Oswiecim on December 18, 1943.

Page 46 TO OLGA

The poem is preserved in manuscript, written in pencil on a scrap of lined paper. It is not signed; at the end of the poem is the number of one of the children's homes, "L 410". From the handwriting and style, it was probably written by Alena Synková (for biographical data, see above).

Pages 48 and 49 FORGOTTEN

The poem is preserved in manuscript, written in pen on a square piece of paper torn from a notebook. There is a spelling error in the title. All other information is missing.

Page 50 THE GARDEN

The poem is preserved in manuscript, probably a copy, together with seven other poems. There is the signature, "Franta Bass", on the right side.

František Bass was born in Brno on September 4, 1930, deported to Terezín on December 2, 1942, and died in Oswiecim on October 28, 1944.

Page 53 ON A SUNNY EVENING

The poem is preserved in a typewritten copy. There is the date "1944" in the upper right corner. No more facts available.

Pages 54 and 55 BIRDSONG

The poem is preserved in manuscript, written in pen on a sheet of white paper together with the poem, "Night in the Ghetto" (see page 42).

Page 56 POOR THING

The poem is preserved in manuscript, written in pen on a square piece of paper torn from a notebook, together with three other poems. Judging from the handwriting and the paper, it is by the same author as the poem, "Forgotten" (see pages 48 and 49).

TIME-TABLE

1939 *March 15*	German Wehrmacht enters Prague. Establishment of Protectorate of Bohemia and Moravia. Up to this time, Jewish children attended the state elementary schools.
July 26	"Zentralstelle für Auswanderung der Juden" set up. A census of Jewish inhabitants was immediately begun according to racial law.
December 1	Jewish children excluded from state elementary schools.
1940 *June 14*	Oswiecim concentration camp set up.
1941 *September 27*	Reinhard Heydrich named acting Reichsprotector. One of his first acts was to order the mass deportation of Jews and the establishment of Terezín as a Jewish ghetto.
October 16	First transport leaves Prague for Lodž ghetto. Among them were children.
October 19	Terezín turned into a Jewish ghetto. In 1930, it had 7,181 inhabitants, half of whom were military personnel living in 11 barracks.
1942 *from January 9 to October 26*	Transports begin to leave for eastern destinations, averaging 1,000 people, among them children. Of these, one percent came back.
August 31	Terezín had a population of 41,552 prisoners. There was 1.6 m^2 of space for each person. The average work week was from 80 to 100 hours. Children from the age of 14 were subject to compulsory labor the same as adults. From 106 to 156 persons died every day.
December 6	There were 3,541 children living in Terezín, 2,000 of whom lived in children's "homes".
1943 *December 31*	3,367 children in Terezín, 1,969 living in children's "homes".
1944 *December 31*	819 children were counted at Terezín under the age of 15 years.
1945 *May 7*	Terezín liberated by Soviet Army.

A total of around 15,000 children under the age of 15 passed through Terezín. Of these, around 100 came back.

"CHILDREN'S DRAWINGS AND POEMS
TEREZÍN 1942–1944"
Edited by Hana Volavková
Translated into English by Jeanne Němcová
Introduction written by Jiří Weil
Catalog collected by Olga Herbenová
Graphic presentation by Karel Pánek
The book was originally published in a special edition
for the State Jewish Museum in Prague,
in 1959
Published by Artia
for Schocken Books, Inc.

ISBN 0-8052-0598-5
1/99/21/51-3

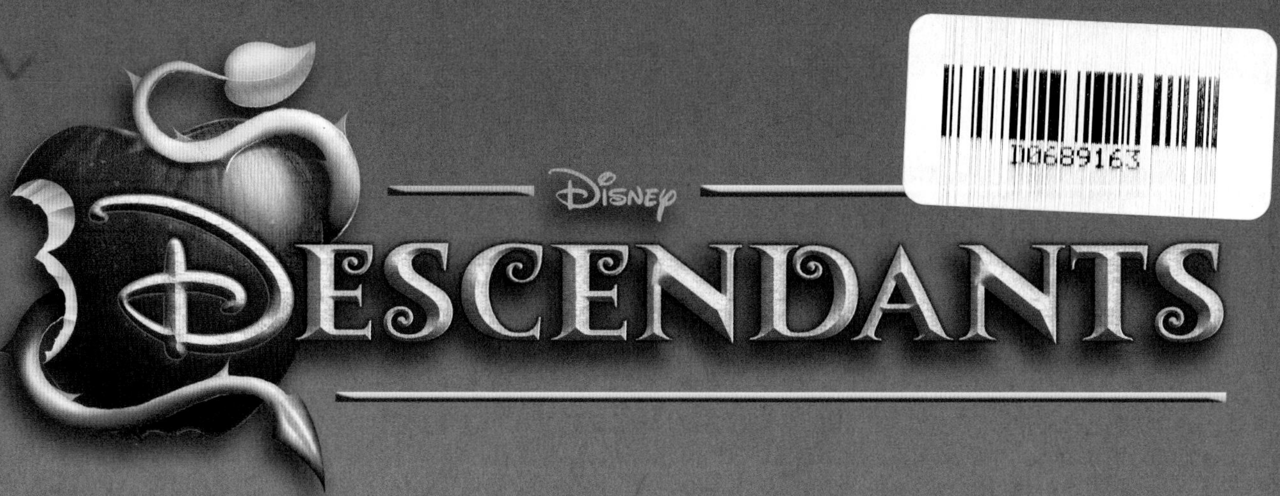

YEARBOOK

Based on the Disney Channel Original Movie

TIME INC. BOOKS
PUBLISHER Margot Schupf
ASSOCIATE PUBLISHER Allison Devlin
VICE PRESIDENT, FINANCE Terri Lombardi
EXECUTIVE DIRECTOR, MARKETING SERVICES Carol Pittard
EXECUTIVE DIRECTOR, BUSINESS DEVELOPMENT Suzanne Albert
EXECUTIVE PUBLISHING DIRECTOR Megan Pearlman
FINANCE DIRECTOR Kevin Harrington
ASSOCIATE DIRECTOR OF PUBLICITY Courtney Greenhalgh
ASSISTANT GENERAL COUNSEL Andrew Goldberg
ASSISTANT DIRECTOR, SPECIAL SALES Ilene Schreider
ASSISTANT DIRECTOR, PRODUCTION Susan Chodakiewicz
SENIOR MANAGER, SALES MARKETING Danielle Costa
SENIOR MANAGER, CHILDREN'S CATEGORY MARKETING Amanda Lipnick
SENIOR MANAGER, BUSINESS DEVELOPMENT + PARTNERSHIPS Nina Fleishman Reed
MANAGER, BUSINESS DEVELOPMENT + PARTNERSHIPS Stephanie Braga
ASSOCIATE PREPRESS MANAGER Alex Voznesenskiy
ASSISTANT PROJECT MANAGER Hillary Leary

EDITORIAL DIRECTOR Stephen Koepp
EXECUTIVE EDITOR, CHILDREN'S BOOKS Beth Sutinis
ART DIRECTOR Gary Stewart
ART DIRECTOR, CHILDREN'S BOOKS Georgia Morrissey
EDITORIAL OPERATIONS DIRECTOR Jamie Roth Major
SENIOR EDITOR Alyssa Smith
ASSISTANT ART DIRECTOR Anne-Michelle Gallero
EDITOR, CHILDREN'S BOOKS Jonathan White
COPY CHIEF Rina Bander
ASSISTANT MANAGING EDITOR Gina Scauzillo
EDITORIAL ASSISTANT Courtney Mifsud

PRODUCED BY DOWNTOWN BOOKWORKS INC.
PRESIDENT Julie Merberg
EDITORIAL DIRECTOR Sarah Parvis
EDITORIAL ASSISTANT Sara DiSalvo
COVER AND INTERIOR DESIGN Georgia Rucker

SPECIAL THANKS: Chelsea Alon, Allyson Angle, Curt Baker, Katherine Barnet, Brad Beatson, Jeremy Biloon, Ian Chin, Rose Cirrincione, Pat Datta, Nicole Fisher, Alison Foster, Joan L. Garrison, Erika Hawxhurst, Kristina Jutzi, David Kahn, Jean Kennedy, Amy Mangus, Melissa Presti, Babette Ross, Dave Rozzelle, Kelsey Smith, Larry Wicker, Krista Wong

Published by Time Inc. Books
225 Liberty Street • New York, NY 10281

ISBN 10: 1-61893-426-0
ISBN 13: 978-1-61893-426-0

We welcome your comments and suggestions about Time Inc. Books
Please write to us at:
Time Inc. Books, Attention: Book Editors, P.O. Box 62310, Tampa, FL 33662-2310
If you would like to order any of our hardcover Collector's Edition books, please call us at 800-327-6388, Monday through Friday, 7 a.m.–9 p.m. Central Time.

1 QGV 15

Congratulations on another marvelous year! From welcoming a new batch of students to enjoying nail-biting action on the tourney field and witnessing an unforgettable coronation, there hasn't been a dull moment here at Auradon Prep! It has been a pleasure to watch each and every one of you grow and learn.

—*Fairy Godmother, Headmistress*

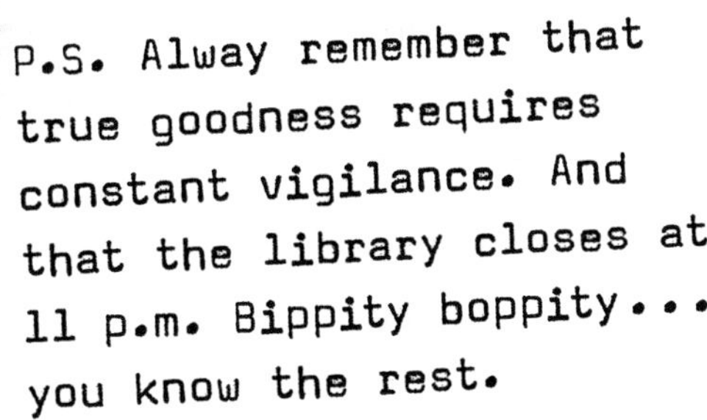

P.S. Alway remember that true goodness requires constant vigilance. And that the library closes at 11 p.m. Bippity boppity... you know the rest.

HIGHLIGHTS

from an Enchanting Year...

Student profiles start on page 10.

Where will we be in 10 years? Check out the career predictions on page 30.

Which subject won the annual favorite class poll? Go to page 32.

What goes on after classes? See pages 34–39.

Tourney rocks! Go, Fighting Knights! Turn to page 36.

Students open up about the things that irk them most. Go to page 40.

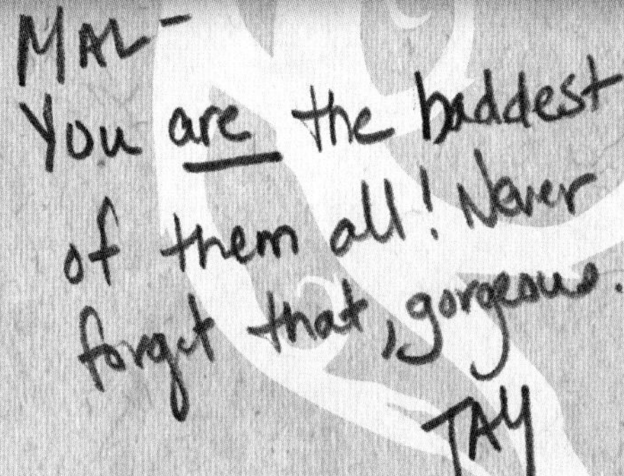

Pretty in pink? Dapper in blue? Learn all about Auradon style on pages 46–51.

Biggest gossip? Most artistic? Find out who took the top honors on page 58.

THE YEAR *in Review*

It's been a big year for Auradon Prep, complete with new students, new classes, and even a new king! Here's a look at just a few of the moments from the past year.

Some HIGHS

Some LOWS

Note passing, roughhousing, and garden spats, oh my!

New Year, NEW STUDENTS

Auradon Prep was proud to welcome some new students this year. Mal, Evie, Jay, and Carlos transferred in, straight from the infamous Isle of the Lost. This fearsome foursome made our student body more fashionable and our tourney team more victorious. They also made our school year more . . . um . . . memorable than we could have imagined.

Jay and Carlos make an unforgettable entrance on their first day.

WATCH YOUR STEP!

Mal and Evie survey the scene.

Ben and Audrey are all smiles as they greet the newest members of the Auradon Prep student body.

Ben extends a hand of welcome to the children of the Isle of the Lost.

Meet
MAL
FAMOUS PARENT: Maleficent
CLOSEST COHORT: Evie
FAVORITES: Drawing, strawberries, hatching dastardly plots
SECRET WISH: To learn how to swim
NOT-SO-SECRET WISH: To have a different middle name
WOULD NEVER LEAVE THE HOUSE WITHOUT: Her magic spell book, her attitude
Stay good!!

Move over, Snow White. Mal is making magic in the kitchen!

I LIKE TO MAKE AN ENTRANCE. –*Mal*

Mal and Jay take a moment between classes.

Purple is this season's hottest color, thanks in part to Mal's stunning wardrobe.

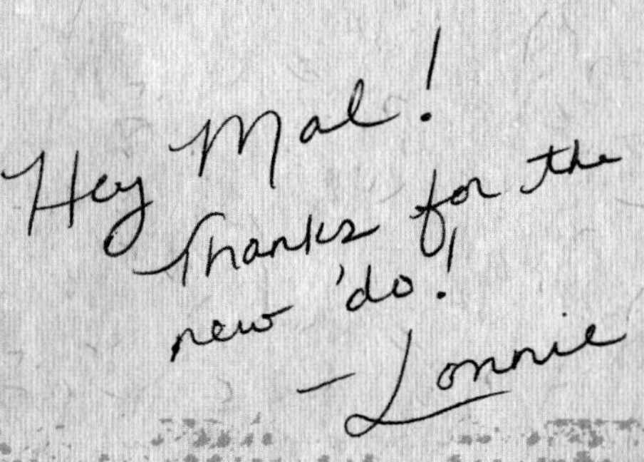

Introducing EVIE

FAMOUS PARENT: The Evil Queen

CLOSEST COHORT: Mal

FAVORITES: Flirting, apples, sewing

SECRET WISH: To ace chemistry

NOT-SO-SECRET WISH: To live in a giant castle with lots of mirrors and a gorgeous prince who loves her

WOULD NEVER LEAVE THE HOUSE WITHOUT: Her purse, a compact, her special mirror, a killer smile

I DON'T GET MAD, I GET EVIE. –Evie

Evie takes over the keyboard for an after-school study session at Carlos and Jay's room. Popcorn for everyone!

Besties Evie and Mal take Remedial Goodness by storm.

Evie shows off her singular style with her ruffle-necked T-shirt and sparkling heart pendant.

Evie and Doug are unstoppable on the dance floor!

Dearest Mal,
You are like a sister to me. I couldn't have survived life on the Isle without you.
-Evie

P.S. - Remember—when applying blush, always use upward strokes!

Get to Know JAY

FAMOUS PARENT: Jafar

CLOSEST COHORT: Carlos

FAVORITES: Winning, victory pizza

SECRET WISH: For his father to be a very successful businessman and never have to work again

NOT-SO-SECRET WISH: To be on a winning tourney team

WOULD NEVER LEAVE THE HOUSE WITHOUT: His charm

Go! Fighting Knights!

Coach Jenkins welcomes Jay to the team.

LADIES' MAN

Jay holds court in the courtyard.

Close-Up on CARLOS

FAMOUS PARENT: Cruella De Vil

CLOSEST COHORTS: Jay, Dude, Ben

FAVORITES: Giving Dude belly rubs, good friends, video games

SECRET WISH: To run a rescue shelter for abused and abandoned animals (and children)

NOT-SO-SECRET WISH: To never see a fur coat or a bunion ever again

WOULD NEVER LEAVE THE HOUSE WITHOUT: An escape route in mind

YOU AIN'T SEEN NOTHIN' YET. –Carlos

ISLE RULES!
x
→ CARLOS

Hear Carlos roar on the tourney field!

HEAR ME ROAR!

Carlos and Jane sure know how to set it off!

No one rocks Isle style like Carlos and Jay!

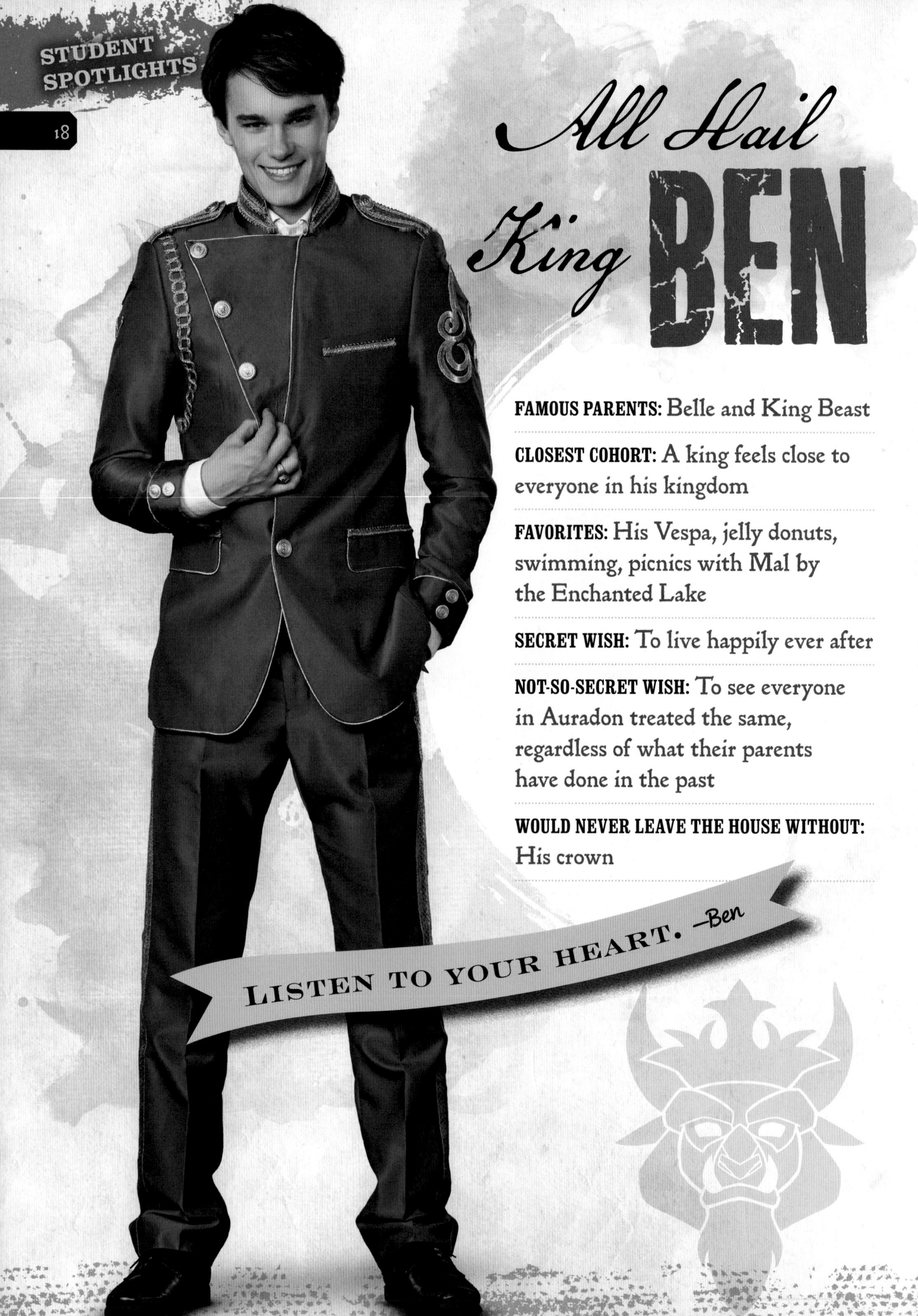

All Hail King BEN

FAMOUS PARENTS: Belle and King Beast

CLOSEST COHORT: A king feels close to everyone in his kingdom

FAVORITES: His Vespa, jelly donuts, swimming, picnics with Mal by the Enchanted Lake

SECRET WISH: To live happily ever after

NOT-SO-SECRET WISH: To see everyone in Auradon treated the same, regardless of what their parents have done in the past

WOULD NEVER LEAVE THE HOUSE WITHOUT: His crown

Mal and Ben preside over an unforgettable post-coronation bash.

A picnic with Ben is a real treat.

Being royal comes with some serious perks!

The Audacious AUDREY

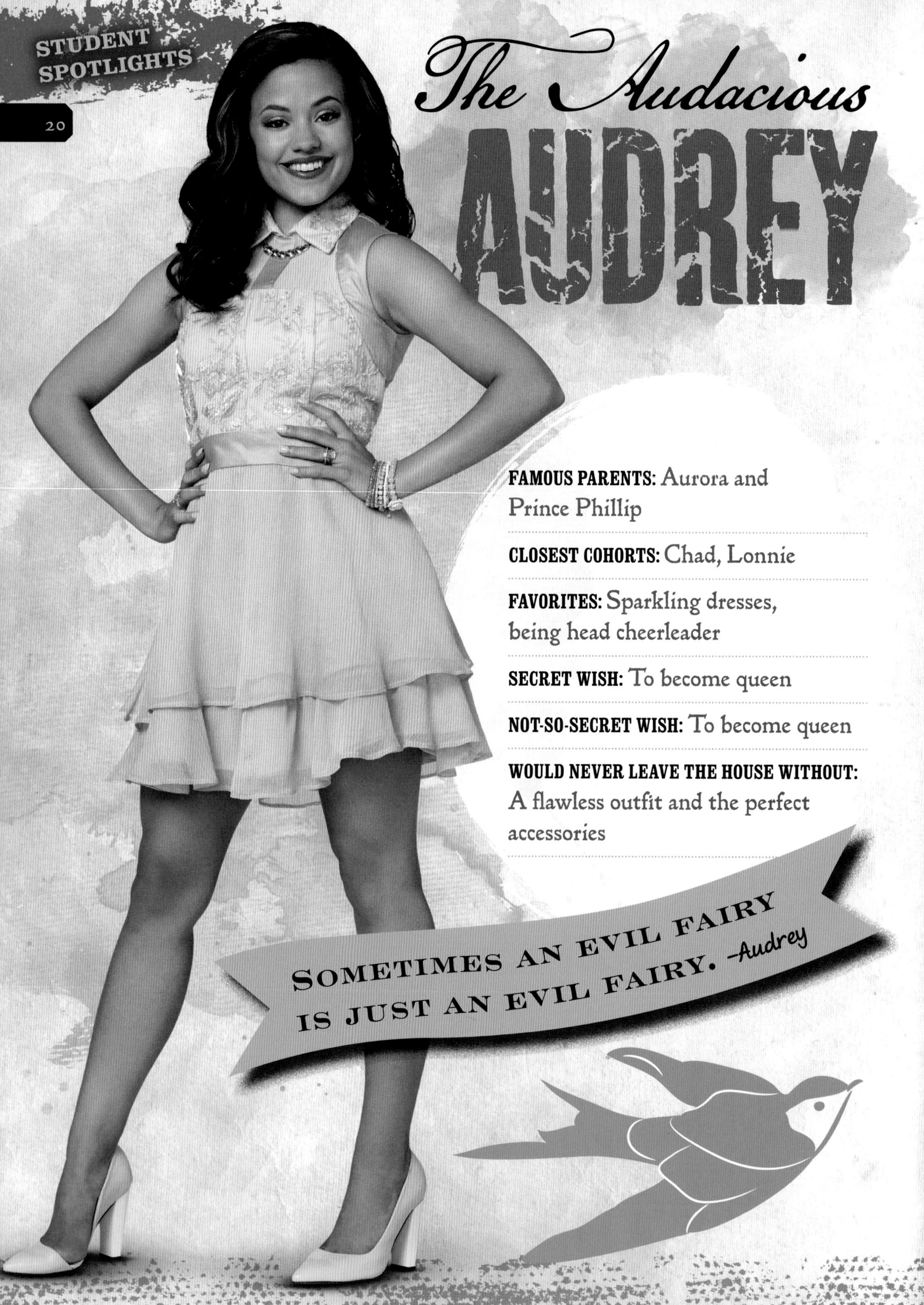

FAMOUS PARENTS: Aurora and Prince Phillip

CLOSEST COHORTS: Chad, Lonnie

FAVORITES: Sparkling dresses, being head cheerleader

SECRET WISH: To become queen

NOT-SO-SECRET WISH: To become queen

WOULD NEVER LEAVE THE HOUSE WITHOUT: A flawless outfit and the perfect accessories

SOMETIMES AN EVIL FAIRY IS JUST AN EVIL FAIRY. –Audrey

Ben, Chad, and Audrey are the epitome of Auradon cool.

Audrey and Ben lead the way when the new students arrive from the Isle of the Lost.

Thanks for not letting your mom
take over the world and stuff.
That was pretty cool of you.
—Audrey

The Unstoppable CHAD Charming

FAMOUS PARENTS: Cinderella and Prince Charming

CLOSEST COHORTS: Audrey, the guys from the tourney team

FAVORITES: Playing tourney, taking selfies

SECRET WISH: To be liked by all the students, even the new kids

NOT-SO-SECRET WISH: To never have to do homework again

WOULD NEVER LEAVE THE HOUSE WITHOUT: Making sure his hair is perfect

Evie and Chad share a moment by the bleachers.

It was a tough day on the tourney grounds for Chad!

Presenting LONNIE!

FAMOUS PARENT: Mulan

CLOSEST COHORT: Audrey

FAVORITES: Long talks with her mom; satin clothes—they're just so shiny!

SECRET WISH: For everyone to be as happy as she is

NOT-SO-SECRET WISH: To be the most fashion-forward girl at Auradon Prep

WOULD NEVER LEAVE THE HOUSE WITHOUT: Her bracelets

CHOCOLATE CHIPS ARE THE MOST IMPORTANT FOOD GROUP. —*Lonnie*

Remember when Lonnie had bangs? Short hair or long, she always looks incredible!

Audrey, Lonnie, and Ben show off their school spirit on Family Day!

Calling all cookie lovers! Meet us in the kitchen for some late-night munchies!

Here's DOUG!

FAMOUS PARENT: Dopey

CLOSEST COHORTS: Evie, the guys from the band

FAVORITES: Band practice, studying with Evie

SECRET WISH: To be a rock star

NOT-SO-SECRET WISH: To spend more time with Evie

WOULD NEVER LEAVE THE HOUSE WITHOUT: His glasses

HI HO. *–Doug*

Lunchtime is the perfect time for Doug and Evie to dish.

Hi Mal,
It was great getting to know you and Evie this year. Especially Evie. Have a fun summer!
—Doug

Doug's a perfect gentleman, on the dance floor and off!

A quick chat with Evie between classes brings a smile to Doug's face.

Spotlight on JANE

FAMOUS PARENT: Fairy Godmother

FAVORITES: Hanging out with Mal, being the tourney mascot

SECRET WISH: To have a boyfriend who loves her

NOT-SO-SECRET WISH: To only have good hair days forever

WOULD NEVER LEAVE THE HOUSE WITHOUT: A bow

The second-floor girls' bathroom doubles as a hair salon when Jane and Mal get together.

DOUBLE TROUBLE

This enchanted family looks enchanting in purple!

Jane slips into Remedial Goodness class for a quick chat with her headmistress...er... mom.

What Will You Be WHEN YOU GROW UP?

CARLOS:
Dog walker or app designer

BEN:
King, founder of a nonprofit that helps the formerly evil

EVIE:
Fashion designer or scientist

JAY:
Professional tourney player, then coach

LONNIE:
Host of a talk show about food, family, and culture
AUDREY:
CEO of a Royal 500 company
CHAD:
Racecar driver, trophy husband
MAL:
Artist

Supreme SUBJECTS

Bad Fairies and Dragon Anatomy usually rank high in our annual poll of students' favorite classes. Let's see how this year's courses stack up.

TOP 10 CLASSES

1. Dragon Anatomy
2. Chemistry
3. Bad Fairies
4. Enchanted Forestry
5. Heroism
6. History of Woodsmen and Pirates
7. Mathematics
8. Basic Chivalry
9. Remedial Goodness 101
10. History of Auradon

Fairy Godmother brings her special brand of bippity boppity boo to this year's newest course offering, Remedial Goodness 101.

CARLOS: History of Woodsmen and Pirates. There are very few dogs in those subjects. Not too many parents either.

EVIE: Chemistry. It turns out I'm great at it. Who doesn't like to shine?

DOUG: Chemistry. I sit next to Evie.

What's Your Favorite Class?

MAL: Remedial Goodness 101. The class is a breeze. I just think of what my mom would do, then pick the opposite.

CHAD: Heroism. I mean, it's what I am destined for. Herotown, population: me. Am I right?

JAY: Basic Chivalry, because . . . hello, ladies.

Head cheerleader Audrey helps her squad reach new heights.

After-School ADVENTURES

When classes wind down for the day, the Auradon Prep campus becomes a flurry of activity. The tourney team heads to the field to start running laps and dodging balls in the kill zone. And while the cheerleaders perfect their pyramids and tosses, the marching band warms up.

Chad and Jay go head-to-head in a heated tourney scrimmage.

With the help of his trusty stopwatch, Ben looks to see if Carlos is the next Auradon Prep track star!

Doug takes a break from band practice to meet the young ladies from the Isle of the Lost.

It's TOURNEY TIME!

The Auradon Prep Fighting Knights are always ready for action on the playing field. Team captain Ben has led the Knights to victory over the Falcons for three years (and counting!). This year's newest players, Jay and Carlos, didn't waste anytime becoming indispensible members of the team.

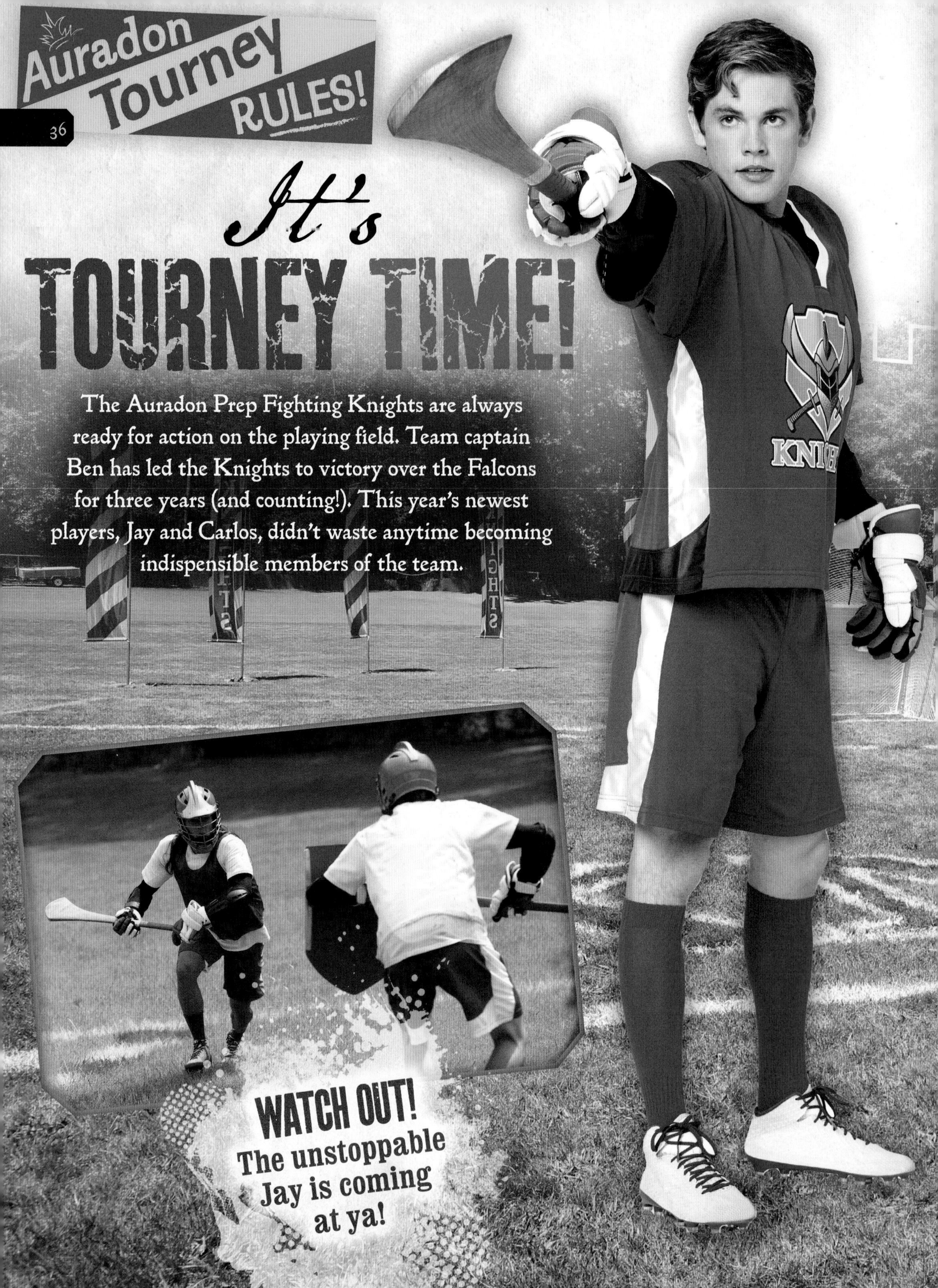

WATCH OUT!
The unstoppable Jay is coming at ya!

TEAM CAPTAIN:
Ben

BIGGEST RIVAL:
Falcons

MOST IMPROVED PLAYER:
Carlos

TEAM LINEUP

Ben	7
Jay	8
Carlos	101
Chad	23
Aziz	11
Brendan	20
Miguel	44
Tyrone	32
Akio	42
William	12

DORM LIFE

When classes are over and activities are done for the day, the students retire to their dorms for studying, sketching, chatting, and, occasionally, plotting world domination. Every dorm on campus has its own distinct style and design.

King Beast and Belle swing by the royal dorm room to visit their son, Ben.

Jay shares his notes with Carlos.

TOP 5 COOLEST THINGS IN BEN'S ROOM

1. Drum kit
2. Exercise equipment
3. Trophy collection
4. Foosball table
5. Framed concert posters

On artsy evenings chèz Mal and Evie, you'll find Mal drawing, Evie whipping up new fashion-forward creations with her sewing machine, and students dropping by for haircuts and styling tips.

Even Dude makes himself at home in Mal and Evie's room!

Check out some of Mal's drawings!

What's your Biggest PET PEEVE?

AUDREY: Evil fairies, boyfriend stealers

Don't forget me. —CHAD

CHAD: Not getting my way

JANE: Being ignored, bad hair days

Family Day

One of the year's most special events brings parents and students together for a day of delicious food, enchanting games, and tons of fun. On Family Day, parents and siblings of current students are invited (if they can travel, that is) to campus for a daylong celebration. It's a tradition—and a treat!

The royal family poses for a Family Day photo!

The annual croquet match draws an impressive crowd.

Hey, Carlos! Hey, Jay! Leave some chocolate-covered strawberries for the rest of us!

Jay, Carlos, Dude, and Evie live it up on Family Day!

Campus CANDIDS

Auradon Prep is more than your average school. It is home to enchanted statues and unforgettable artwork. A quick walk across campus makes it clear to students and visitors alike that our school is a very special place with a real sense of magic, history, and tradition . . . and goofy students doing ridiculous things.

NEED A NAPKIN?

Um, Carlos. You've got a little something on your face.

Evie shows off her royal curtsy.

LUNCHTIME FAIL!

Looks like someone doesn't like her lunch!

As the spellbinding statue of King Beast morphs from beast to man and back again, some students are awestruck. And others are just plain spooked!

"Hold on for a sec. I really need to take this."

THIS IS WHAT THEY'RE COOKING UP IN THE KITCHEN?

Even four-legged Fighting Knights know how to live it up at Auradon Prep!

Between classes, gal pals can always be found gabbing in the ladies' room.

Jay says he will crush the competition.

TRENDSETTERS

Every year, students bring their own brand of cool to the halls of Auradon Prep. Last year, pastels and cashmere ruled the school. But this year, an influx of Isle style brought edgier colors and fabrics to our fair shores. See which styles stood out the most.

Doug brings back the bow tie!

It looks like leather gloves are all the rage on the Isle of the Lost. Will they survive the transition to the mainland? Here's hoping.

This is not your grandmother's cape sleeve! Evie has transformed the flowing cape look from "once upon a time" into "hip here and now."

Extra zippers take these outfits up a notch on the punk-rock scale.

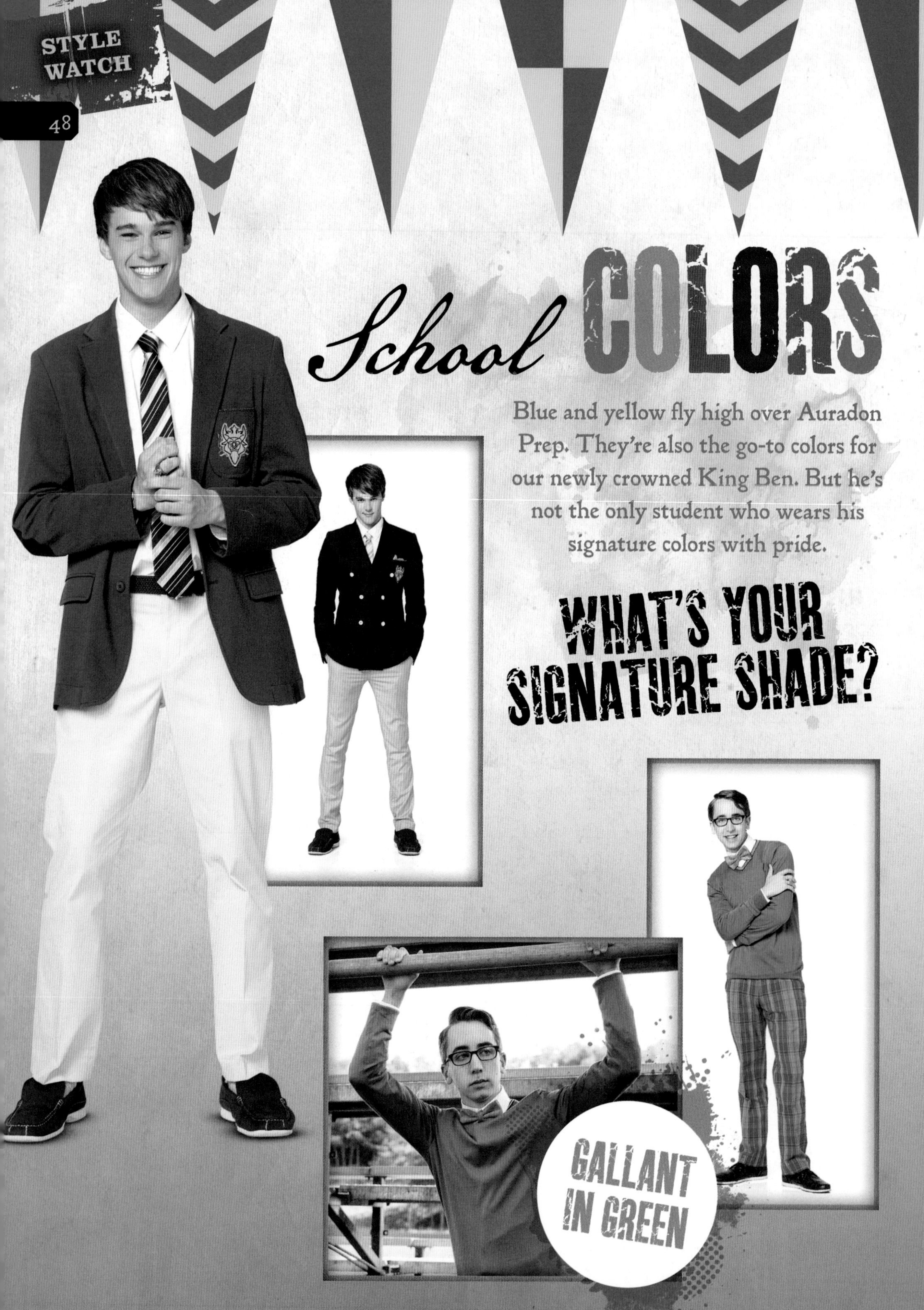

School COLORS

Blue and yellow fly high over Auradon Prep. They're also the go-to colors for our newly crowned King Ben. But he's not the only student who wears his signature colors with pride.

WHAT'S YOUR SIGNATURE SHADE?

GALLANT IN GREEN

PURPLE
PIZZAZZ!

TRUE
BLUE!

A VISION
IN PINK

BLACK
AND WHITE...
AND DASHING
ALL OVER!

Auradon Girls Know How to ACCESSORIZE!

As Snow White always says, "Accessories make the outfit." Here at Auradon Prep, the students never miss a chance to add some bling to a fairy-tale ensemble. Here are a few standouts.

Lonnie could easily be crowned Queen of the Headband.

Elegant and regal, Evie's tiaras are fit for a princess.

Jane is never fully dressed without a bow (or four or five)!

STYLE SHOWDOWN

Can you match these awesome accessories to the correct fashionista?

1. EVIE OR AUDREY? Match these purses to their stylish owners.

A.

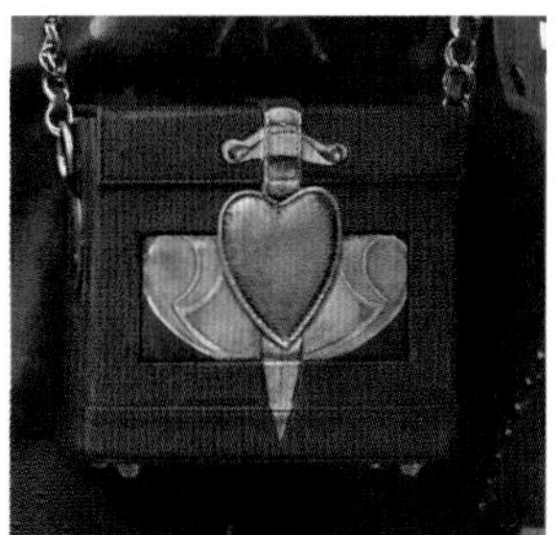

B.

C.

D.

2. LONNIE OR JANE? Can you place these pairs on the correct feet?

A.

B.

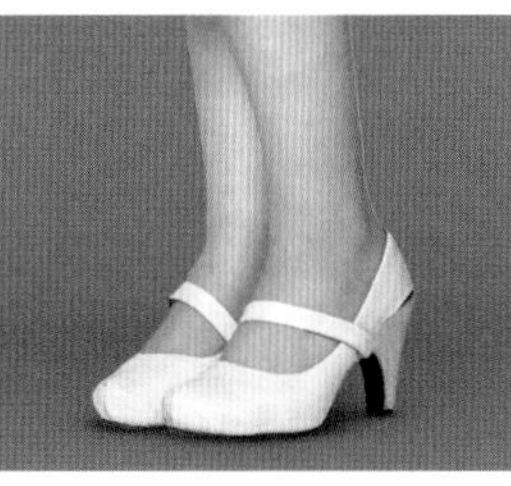

C.

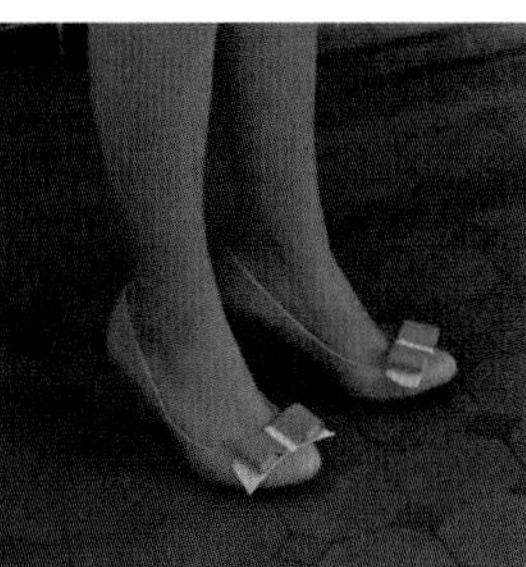

D.

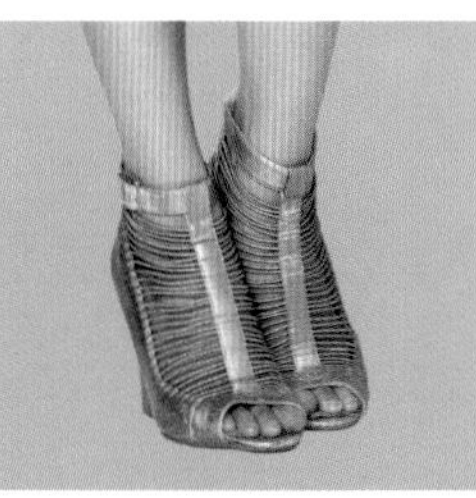

3. MAL OR EVIE? Which pieces of jewelry belong to which stylish student?

A.

B.

C.

D.

Style Showdown Answers:

1. Evie: A, D. Audrey: B, C. 2. Lonnie: A, D. Jane: B, C. 3. Mal: B, D. Evie: A, C.

What Makes You UNIQUE?

Look around at your classmates. Who is most likely to speak at graduation? Who is most likely to toilet paper the King's castle? Who is most likely to invent a usable jetpack to get to tourney practice faster?

Make a prediction! Fill in the blanks for yourself and your friends.

JAY
MOST LIKELY TO... Take two girls to prom!

MAL
MOST LIKELY TO... Be caught stealing candy from a baby ... and giving it back.

BEN
MOST LIKELY TO... RULE MY HEART!

CARLOS
MOST LIKELY TO... break into the pound and set all of the animals free

DOUG
MOST LIKELY TO... Invent a really cool ROBOT

EVIE
MOST LIKELY TO... Be late for class because she's redesigning her outfit

CHAD
MOST LIKELY TO... Install mirrors in every room of his house

Museum of WONDERS

Sometimes you really need to know about the order of succession in the Great Goblin Kingdom, and other times you might just want to marvel at the glittery jewels in the Crowns of Auradon exhibit. Whether it is for a class or just for fun, we are so lucky to have the Museum of Cultural History just around the corner!

Fairy Godmother's wand is the star attraction of its very own gallery at the Museum of Cultural History.

The entrance atrium of the museum inspires awe in its many visitors.

What's Your Go-To Object at the Museum?

Cinderella's glass slipper? King Triton's trident? The magic lamp? Of all the amazing artifacts in the Museum of Cultural History, which one do you think is the coolest?

CARLOS: I like to check out D'Artagnan's sword, hat, and boots. D'Artagnan was one brave guy. I really look up to him. Maybe I should start carrying a sword . . .

MAL: The magic spinning wheel. It looks so boring, but it's kind of spooky that a few pieces of wood could put someone to sleep for 100 years.

EVIE: Whenever I am in the museum (and I can assure you I've only been there during daytime hours), I stop by King Beast's Mystical Rose. It's really beautiful. I'd love for a prince to give me an enchanted rose some day. Well, 12 of them. A whole bouquet of roses would be way better than one measly magical rose. I'm just saying.

JANE: I used to visit my mom's wand a lot. I don't do that anymore.

Gallery of Villains

TOP 5 FAVORITE GALLERIES

Once again, the Gallery of Villains came out on top of our annual poll of the students' most-visited rooms in the Museum of Cultural History.

1. Gallery of Villains
2. Gallery of Enchanted Armor
3. Hall of Swords
4. Kingdoms Under the Sea
5. Gallery of Dwarves, Gnomes, and Goblins

FIELD TRIP!

Auradon Prep alumni never forget their trips off campus to Camelot, Charmington, Fortuna, or Belle's Harbor. There's a lot of history to be found all around the United States of Auradon. For a truly relaxing day enveloped in the magic of nature, you don't have to go all the way to Sherwood Forest. You can pop over to our beloved Enchanted Lake.

The Enchanted Lake brings out the Zen in everyone—even Mal!

With a beautiful bridge over a rushing stream and a lush green forest surrounding a tranquil lake, a visit to the Enchanted Lake is the perfect afternoon getaway.

Mal—
My world changed the moment I met you. I am the luckiest guy in Auradon.
Love you,
Ben
P.S. Thanks for listening to your heart!

Auradon's #1 couple enjoy a lakeside picnic.

TOP 5 MOST POPULAR DAY TRIPS

Spooky old Skull Island knocked the glamorous court in Cinderellasburg out of the top spot this year.

1. Skull Island
2. Rocky Point Court in Cinderellasburg
3. Grimmsville
4. Neverland
5. Belle's Harbor on the Strait of Ursula

THE VOTES ARE IN!

Biggest Flirt
Most Artistic
Biggest Gossip

A Royal CELEBRATION!

Class projects, exams, all-night study sessions, late-night gossip, weekend trips to Neverland . . . What a whirlwind year! But the event of the year of was, without a doubt, the coronation. People, young and old, came from every corner of the United States of Auradon to see Ben don his royal crown for the very first time.

WE DO NOT BECOME GREAT BY OUR STRENGTH BUT BY OUR COMPASSION! -Ben

Ben and Mal share a quiet moment in the carriage on the way to the cathedral for the coronation.

Ben admits that he was both nervous and excited before he spoke his oath.

A CROWN FIT FOR A KING!

The coronation was an action-packed event, complete with an unforgettable, fire-breathing surprise guest and some shocking revelations. But at the end of the day, what's most important is that Ben spoke the oath that makes him king and that everyone in the realm stayed safe. Phew! All's well that ends well in Auradon!

I solemnly swear to govern the Peoples of Auradon with justice and mercy as long as I reign.

SET IT OFF!

The Coronation Ball was a once-in-a-lifetime event here in Auradon. When the lights went down and the music came up, our students did not disappoint on the dance floor!

Write the book—the story of our lives.

Rock this beat.

Be yourself. Forget the DNA.

We got the keys.
The kingdom's ours!

Start a chain reaction. Never let it stop!

SO LONG!
SEE YOU NEXT YEAR . . .